17

Cricket in the Leagues

CRICKET
in the Leagues

John Kay

with a Foreword by Learie Constantine

EYRE & SPOTTISWOODE
LONDON

First Published 1970
© *1970 John Kay*
Printed in Great Britain on behalf of
Eyre & Spottiswoode (Publishers). Ltd.
11 New Fetter Lane, E.C.4
by The Bowering Press, Plymouth
SBN 413 27370 9

to
ELSIE who has seen it all happen and
for
JONATHAN to whom the future beckons

Contents

Plates

ACKNOWLEDGEMENTS for photographs are due to the *Manchester
Evening News* for Plates, 6, 11, 17, *Bradford Telegraph* and *Argus*,
Plates 9 and 19, The *Daily Herald*, Plate 12, *Sport and General*,
Plate 14, P.A. Reuters, Plate 16, T. H. Pratt, Esq., Plate 20, Press
Association, Plates 24 and 25, United Press International (U.K.),
Plate 26, *Birmingham Post and Mail*, Plate 30. For supplying all
other photographs the publisher is grateful to the author.

Foreword

By Learie Constantine

JOHN KAY is a sports writer. More than that, he is a dedicated follower of cricket – League cricket, and in this book he has assembled the most comprehensive picture of cricket in the Leagues – England, Scotland, Wales. I have noted the omission of Ireland. I have myself coached Trinity College and although the Irishman plays his cricket keenly and with a lot of fury, the clubs are not of a standard to compete on even terms with the north of England clubs that John Kay is discussing ih this book. But it was only last year, 1969, that Ireland comprehensively defeated the West Indies Touring team in a one-day match.

To close followers of the game I believe we are on common ground when I say that the three Leagues that matter are, the Central Lancashire, Bradford and Lancashire. There are other Leagues competing for a place in the sun, but Staffordshire, for instance, even in the great days of Syd Barnes, Aaron Lockett, Dick Tyldesley did not enjoy the publicity and interest enjoyed by those I have mentioned.

John Kay writes, and it is worth repeating,

'The Lancashire League like the Central started off with four main objectives (1) To promote a greater interest in the game (2) To foster and develop amateur talent. (3) To inspire punctuality in the matches and to arrange an annual competition among its members and (4) To control professionalism.'

The distinction between the amateur and professional having been destroyed, many are the writers who are trying to re-introduce the class barrier among the players by a new use of the word 'Professional'. But let me quote John Kay again: 'In the beginning when clubs were frequently permitted to engage two professionals, one a batsman, the other a bowler, the underlying principle of professionalism in League Cricket was to employ men whose task was not to produce match-winning figures with bat or ball, but to serve the best interests of their club by preparing the right type of pitches and by teaching at all times the basic essentials of how to play Cricket.' How have times changed?

The happy mind which John Kay has brought into writing this book is easily passed to the reader. It is not a history of League Cricket. It is not, says John Kay, a catalogue of clubs and players, or leagues and associations. It is simply the story of what lies behind League Cricket and what makes it such a fascinating game.

It has taken players in the south of England a long time to realize that the northern League matches were not a series of 'dog fights'. Now that the spirit is spreading in the south, John Kay's book could not have been better timed.

The book omits no-one. The administrator, the groundsman, the young boys, the village or town folk who turn up evening after evening to see, to help and to glory in the success of the team, they are all here. I only hope they enjoy reading the book with the same degree of joy that I enjoyed reading the manuscript. I recommend it wholeheartedly.

Introduction

League cricket is club cricket spiced by competition and stream-lined by rules and regulations. It flourishes in Lancashire and Yorkshire but is also played in the North, the South, the East, and the West of England as well as in Scotland and Wales. It embraces professionalism but is not, apart from one or two of the major Lancashire leagues, dominated by it. In the main league cricket is good cricket, keen, competitive and highly entertaining. It demands considerable sacrifice not only by the players but by club officials and those who watch it, either by taking out club membership or paying at the gate match by match.

To the stranger league cricket means mostly big-name pro-fessionals returning fantastic batting and bowling figures and commanding princely salaries for a few hours' work on a Saturday afternoon. In reality, league cricket is amateur cricket. Nowadays, in a difficult economic climate, far more leagues shun profes-sionalism than encourage it. They have no objection to allowing the paid cricketer into their ranks but in face of fierce competition, and there is no real agreement where the counter-attractions start or finish, the majority of cricketing leagues are content to leave the signing of the international cricketer to the biggest and probably the most famous league of all – the Lancashire League.

Here, in a thirty-mile portion of Lancashire, are fourteen clubs, that range from the big towns of Burnley and Blackburn, to the smaller ones of Accrington and Nelson, to the villages of Church and Enfield. It is the proud boast of the Lancashire League followers that only the best players are good enough to become club professionals and certainly the cricketing countries of the world have been scoured to provide the attractions for a cricketing public that looks upon first-class cricket, rightly or wrongly, as only for the privileged few. Year by year the cost of maintaining their world-famous reputation rises and rises but always the battle continues and it cannot be denied that the Lancashire League holds a unique position in the world of cricket.

It has attracted the best players from every cricketing country in the world and in doing so has created something of a false image. The real strength in league cricket lies in its amateur players and its enthusiastic honourary officials. Without their support, on the field and off it, producing runs or taking wickets and, perhaps even more important, raising money to foot the soaring bills, lies a story of sporting sacrifices second to none. There is no money to be made in league cricket, except for the professional and, let it never be forgotten, he is out-numbered ten to one in every team.

Most of the important Lancashire leagues date back to the nineteenth century. The Lancashire League, like its nearby rival, the Central Lancashire League, was founded in 1892 and the aims of both were briefly outlined in four major objects.

To promote a greater interest in the game. To foster and develop amateur talent. To inspire punctuality in the matches and to arrange an annual competition among its members. Fourthly and lastly comes the decision and desire 'to control professionalism'. This will be a surprise to the casual observer but he should not be misled. The Lancashire League in particular controls its professionals rigidly. It standardizes contracts in many ways without interfering with the bargaining ability of its clubs from the financial point of view. It ensures that professionals are available for ALL matches and not just for the important ones and insists that they also coach as well as play. It may well be that with the passage of time there is less emphasis on coaching than is wise and the cynics are not without ammunition when they talk of 'buying' championships by the engagement of the world's best players to dominate the Saturday afternoon cricketing sphere.

Be that as it may. Let no man decry either the standard of play or the spirit in which it is played in leagues generally and in Lancashire and Yorkshire in particular. In the beginning, when clubs were frequently permitted to engage two professionals, one

a batsman, the other a bowler, the underlying principle of professionalism in league cricket was to employ men whose main
task was not to produce match-winning figures with bat or ball,
but to serve the best interests of their clubs by preparing the
right kind of pitches and by teaching at all times the basic essentials of how to play cricket. They were, in the main, groundsmen
and coaches and if this state of affairs no longer persists it is
because of the pressure applied by those who watch and those
who play alongside the professionals of today. I have yet to meet a
league cricket official who is really happy about the present trend
towards overwhelming and over-expensive professionalism.

This book is not a history of league cricket. It is not even a
catalogue of clubs and players or leagues and associations. It is
the story of what lies behind league cricket and, because I was
brought up in the hot-bed that was Central Lancashire League
cricket between two world wars, it is centred around the clubs and
the players, amateurs and professionals, not forgetting the hard-
working men behind the scenes. In Lancashire there is far more
cricket played outside of Old Trafford, the home of the county
side, than there is inside. Even when Lancashire are playing at
home on a Saturday or a Sunday, there are far more people
watching league cricket in a radius of fifty miles or so than there
are at Old Trafford.

And this book is also the story of what makes league cricket
such a fascinating game. As a player for 25 years and an honorary
official for a similar period I gained an extensive knowledge of
what it takes to keep the league game alive. To rub shoulders
with the world-famous professionals in my playing days was a
thrill and a great source of enjoyment, friendship and prestige.
To put back a little into the game when in retirement was also a
pleasure and a privilege but it is only when an innings, on and
off the field, is complete that one really gets the true picture of
cricket played in the leagues. It is no different from the game that
is played elsewhere at club level except, perhaps, that it is better
organized and more strictly controlled. In a word league cricket
is disciplined cricket – but it is not essentially professional cricket.
Far from it.

Part I

Chapter 1

The Man who Inspired

His name was Lionel Cranfield. When he died, just as the 1968 cricket season was about to open, the world of big cricket knew him only as a name. He had played a couple of first-class matches with Gloucestershire before World War I and contributed little to the county cricket scene. Yet, in the leagues of Lancashire, Lionel Cranfield symbolized all that was best in the game. He was a club cricket professional who fulfilled the basic essentials of his employment. He knew how to make grass grow and how to produce a good cricketing pitch. He could bat with both style and power. As a bowler he was a canny spinner, mixing the leg-break with the off-break and frequently sending down a top-spinner that gained him lbw decisions by the dozen season after season. It was often argued that he never bowled a googly. This kindly and shrewd cricketer could not be drawn on that vital aspect of his game. His outlook towards the googly, the most difficult of all cricketing deliveries, was one of plain commonsense. If the batsmen thought he bowled a googly why should he argue differently?

He came to Middleton in the middle 1920s and took unto himself the task of rebuilding a club that had suffered much through the ravages of war. Its leading players had been killed on the battlefield, its finances were at low ebb, and its ground at Towncroft was sadly in need of renovation. But Lionel Cranfield had a florist's shop in the town and he signed for Middleton for less money than he could have obtained elsewhere in league cricket because of the challenge the job offered and the prospect that his engagement might be good for business – the florist business. He had played league cricket before the war and after it in the Central Lancashire League, the Lancashire League and the Bolton League and his fame, at league cricket level, was high. Those who watched league cricket, and they were always a goodly number in those days, reckoned any side that had 'Cranny' as a professional was hard to beat. Certainly he could score runs against the best attacks fielded and dismiss the opposition batsmen as regularly and as cheaply as most of his fellow professionals – and they included such names as S. F. Barnes, C. H. Parkin, C. B. Llewellyn, V. Norbury and P. E. Morfee. The latter was the fastest bowler I ever saw. He came north from Kent and had the longest run of any fast bowler of that decade or this. Yet Lionel Cranfield handled him with consummate ease and stroked his best deliveries past cover or wide of mid-off. On the field 'Cranny' could not be faulted.

Off it he earned the undying gratitude of a group of young and eager schoolboys by taking them under his care to foster and develop a love of cricket that opened up for them a new way of life. Schools cricket in 1924 was a rough and ready business. Any reasonably level stretch of ground, be it turf or cinders, was accepted as a pitch and although the bowler was always the master under these conditions it was the batsmen who gained most renown once Lionel Cranfield spotted them and used his influence to get them 'transferred' across the road to the well-prepared wickets of the town club.

His contract called for him to coach three nights a week. He seldom failed to put in a fourth night's duty and devote it to his boys. He had, of course, to give priority to the senior players and then to those in the second eleven but never a night passed without 'Cranny' instructing four or five youngsters to stay behind and spend the last half-hour spellbound as he taught them the rudiments of batting, bowling and fielding. Admittedly he used a little bribery. In payment for our 'lessons' we were expected to help him pull the heavy roller up and down the pitch he was preparing for the next match; and Saturday's wicket never lacked for preparation. I was one of his pupils. My brother, Edwin, who became one of the league's most prolific and stylish scorers and is now acting as Honorary Secretary of the Central Lancashire League, was another. Jack Wilson, a tall red-haired youngster who could, at the age of fifteen, bowl leg-spinners better than anybody I ever saw, was another. Cranfield's son, Monty, who afterwards went on to join the Lancashire staff at Old Trafford and later played for Gloucestershire, the county of his birth, was also in the group.

We were all in the same school side and if any team managed to obtain more than 20 runs against us Lionel Cranfield wanted to know why! He had taught the bowlers amongst us to pitch a length and our batsmen to play down the line. On the unsympathetic pitches on which matches were played Cranfield was full of praise for a batsman who reached double figures. On the other hand he expected his bowling fledgelings to gain their wickets at three or four runs each.

He pleaded in vain for better facilities for the schoolboy cricketers of the day and as soon as they left school he made sure they were not lost to the game by persuading either their parents or the club committee to make membership possible – even at a cut fee. And so on went the lessons. From six o'clock each evening, Friday, Saturday and Sunday excepted, Cranfield's 'Young Hopefuls' were in attendance at the Middleton nets. The first two hours had to be spent fielding for the seniors and, at the same time, listening and observing the way the old pro went about his job of making ordinary cricketers play just a little bit better. It was not time wasted. When the regulars had finished old Li would turn to us and for the last hour we were in the seventh heaven of cricketing delight. Basically we who aspired to become batsmen had to learn to push down the line, left foot forward and left elbow well up. Those who were more inclined to be bowlers had to master the art of 'clipping' their left or right ear with as straight an arm as possible and to lean into their action in an effort to make the ball 'do things'.

It sounded difficult but Lionel Cranfield would halt the batsman in his shot or the bowler in his stride to demonstrate what he wanted and why it was necessary. His two cardinal principles were for batsmen to keep their head well over the ball and bowlers to bring their arm over as high and as straight as possible. Today they might be described as old-fashioned methods, but they brought results and produced a happy and talented bunch of eager young league cricketers. That none of them went on to make the grade at top level was not Cranfield's fault – simply that the demands of the industrial world and the necessity of earning a living stood in the way. Slowly and surely Cranfield guided his youngsters towards success. His coaching ensured most of the group a place in the Middleton second team as teen-agers and there came the greatest moment of all when the local 'wakes' holidays took several regular first-teamers away from duty. The team had no hope of the championship and the season was fast approaching its end so there was no great pressure brought to bear on the cricketing 'defaulters'. They were allowed to take a match off and Lionel Cranfield pleaded for the inclusion of three of his youngsters against Castleton Moor who had as their professional the one and only Sydney Barnes – to many the greatest bowler of all time. When Cranfield was reminded that his fledgelings would have to face the mighty Barnes he did not demur. 'They will be all the better for the experience,' was his comment.

And so three of us, my brother, Jack Wilson and myself, were roped into service and had to toss up for the last three batting places. Barnes, as usual, was in deadly form. In little more than an hour he had sent back Middleton's first five batsmen for a mere 40 runs or so and three scared young cricketers were about to be thrown in at the deep end. A word from 'Cranny' calmed us down. He told us to do as he had taught us to do – to play forward with head well down, left foot to the pitch of the ball and left elbow bent to keep the ball on the grass. With seven men out for 52 the crisis was reached and Edwin Kay was first to face the music. He did as he was told. So did Jack Wilson and between them they carried the total to 87 in spite of Barnes and the closest set field I had then seen. Eventually Wilson was out. He grew too ambitious and tried to hit Barnes back over his head for a boundary. Call it the courage or the impertinence of youth if you will but do not begrudge a new boy his good intentions. A return catch brought me to the crease and a total of 100 looked a mighty long way distant. But I remembered the Cranfield creed and stuck it out for several overs until the great man bowled me middle stump. I had not scored but Middleton were 99 all out and a kindly old man on the pavilion side patted me on the back as I trudged dismally back to the dressing room. 'Never mind, lad, tha's in good company. Old Syd's bowled out Jack Hobbs before today.' His words were never forgotten and the cheers for my brother, a much better batsman, were music in the ears of all of us. Alas Middleton lost but the day was made complete when the great man himself, Sydney F. Barnes, the cricketer it was often said who had no sense of humour nor any kindness of disposition, popped his head into the Middleton dressing room to single out three sheepish young cricketers and say, 'Well played, you boys – it's easy to see you are Cranny's lads!'

That was the beginning. It was league cricket at its best. Young cricketing upstarts tilting at windmills like the great Sydney Barnes and sharing the applause for a memorable even if modest recovery effort. It was the sort of thing that happened week after week in league cricket and as the years wore on and the emphasis turned from professionals who were primarily groundsmen and coaches to players of world-wide repute the opportunity for the local boy to collar the headlines by hammering a Test match bowler for six or bowling out an international batsman for a duck became more and more apparent.

In time old 'Cranny' moved on. He left Middleton to spread the gospel with still another league club. Season after season he returned batting and bowling figures to match the best; he also held his catches with uncanny certainty and looked, in the field, what he really was – the complete cricketer. But Lionel Cranfield's work off the field and at the practice nets was of even greater significance. With an encouraging word and a helpful display of how to play a shot or deliver a ball he went on his way content to start some youngsters off on the way to cricketing pleasure. As he grew old he still stayed on. When league cricket became too much for him he accepted a position as assistant coach under George Hirst at Eton and continued the good work of teaching cricket to boys with the world at their feet.

He finally came back home to Middleton and was still coaching the younger end at Towncroft when approaching his eightieth year. He could not then take the bat to demonstrate a stroke nor raise his arm high enough to bowl the ball he had in mind but he still got the message through and there would be a twinkle in his eye as he sipped his glass of beer before going home. He had spotted one or two more good boys with what it takes to make a cricketer. When last I spoke to him he was bemoaning the lack of opportunity for the young 'uns. League cricket tended to become overburdened with middle-aged amateurs who were enjoying themselves so much they did not want to retire. He left me to agree with him that, 'there's nothing wrong with cricket if the youngsters are treated right'.

Chapter 2

What Makes a League Club

Success on the field in league cricket calls for a sound professional and a steady supply of good amateur players. Another essential is a captain who can inspire as well as control and, again Middleton, typical of the league clubs just after World War I, were lucky with their leaders as well as their professional. The first skipper of my acquaintance was one Billy Pink, a delightful man and a stylish batsman who batted so low down in the order that he seldom allowed himself the scope for the big score he was capable of. Nonetheless he was the ideal captain – strict enough to demand full-scale attention to the job by both professional and amateurs and human enough to share in the dressing-room banter that was always a feature of a happy club side. It was said of Billy Pink, a cotton salesman and regular church-goer who sang in the local parish church choir, that he never had a wrong word with any man on the field of play. I can well believe it. At the same time I can vouch for the fact that few got the better of him when it came, as quite frequently it did, to a tricky point of cricketing law or etiquette.

The combination of Billy Pink and Lionel Cranfield was the basis on which Middleton built a side that was capable of giving the best teams in the Central Lancashire League a hard game. The side took few honours, winning only one championship in the 1920s but also taking the Wood Cup the first time this crowd-pulling knock-out competition was launched on the instigation of a Middleton man, John Henry Wood, who typified the spirit of league cricket in that period.

Wood had been a player all his life and captained the club from the turn of the century until the outbreak of World War I and for a couple of seasons afterwards. He was never a great player but he was an enthusiastic one and although he combined cricket with a business life centred around the cotton industry as a mill-owner and a mill manager he also was a prominent figure in local politics who still found time not only to play the game but to administrate it.

As Mayor of the Borough he was an automatic President of the town club as well as its captain and in addition he was so highly esteemed in cricketing quarters that he was President of the Central Lancashire League for several lengthy periods. His introduction of the Wood Cup Competition in 1921 as an additional outlet for mid-week cricket was a gesture that brought new life to the League and the Wood Cup became undoubtedly the biggest moneyspinner in years. Alderman Wood remained in charge at Middleton until his death and it is said that on many occasions when funds were low and the bills were placed on the committee room table he would pick them up and ask to be allowed to take them home for further study. They seldom came back. Instead the receipts would flow through and crisis was averted.

His final gesture was typical of a grand sportsman. With the end of the war and the demand for a big rehousing programme uppermost in the minds of the local authorities the Alderman fought a mighty battle on the Town Council to save the Middleton ground at Towncroft from the builders. He lost but was not beaten. He purchased the ground himself and then made it over to the Club in perpetuity and under trusteeship of three senior aldermen with the wish that it remain an open space for ever and, in the unlikely event of the Cricket Club going out of existence, the ground revert to the Borough as a public playing field. Thus the builders were thwarted and cricket consolidated. Alderman John Henry Wood is a name revered not only in Middleton but throughout the Central Lancashire League and although I knew him only as an old man with a gruff voice and a stern attitude to all who did not treat their cricket seriously I learned to appreciate what a sterling character he was when he turned out to fill a holiday gap in the side when well over sixty.

He took over the captaincy for the day and fielded at mid-on and whenever the ball was hit past him he gruffly commanded myself and another youngster filling in as holiday relief 'chase that, son'. At close of play this leading citizen of the town stood in the middle of the dressing room in his cricketing shirt and minus his trousers to order, in the same gruff voice, beer for the men and lemonade for the boys, and as an extra treat bought up the stock of meat pies left behind the bar. He was the salt of the cricketing earth. Every club needed a man of his standing and wisdom to guide them through the rebuilding days that followed the end of World War I and almost without exception they were forthcoming. At Heywood there was Dr Hitchon, a giant of a man who skippered the club, took charge at committee meetings, frequently paid the bills and finally went on to become a leading member and eventually President of the Lancashire County Cricket Club. At Rochdale there was that little financial wizard Jimmy White whose love of cricket was combined with a passion for race horses and the stage and boosted by an amazing career in the world of high finance. At Moorside, a village club on the outskirts of Oldham, it was the Mellodew family, mill-owners and big employers of local labour, who kept the wolf from the door in the bad days and excelled on the field on match days. It was at Moorside, one sunny Saturday afternoon in the early 1920s that a promising teen-age left-hander took the field in short white flannels to help his father, the club professional, put the opposition to rout. His name was Maurice Leyland and he went on to become one of Yorkshire's and England's best players. The men behind the scenes in league cricket were as important as those on it for money was scarce and a new way of life was opening up for the public in their leisure hours.

The names may well be different but the story remained the same wherever you went in league cricket. The professionals, like Lionel Cranfield, were first and foremost the men who taught you how to play the game and combined this cricketing duty with the art of groundsmanship and the making of pitches that were as near perfect as tools and turf permitted. Without good amateur aid the professional had to work hard and long to keep his side in respectability and lucky the paid player who had a good amateur bowler and a couple of good unpaid batsmen to offer aid at all times. At Middleton, I recall, as a starry-eyed schoolboy, seeing Jimmy Ogden capture all ten Oldham wickets one glorious Saturday afternoon in a delightful exhibition of economical swing bowling that looked harmless enough from the boundary edge but never failed to account for a goodly number of batsmen match after match, season after season. Jimmy Ogden was the complete amateur sportsman. He could hold his own with the best in local tennis circles, swim well enough to collar prizes galore at the winter galas, and play golf with such effortless ease that his club colleagues marvelled whenever he strayed off the fairway.

As a boy I marvelled at his control over length and swing but later, when I came to know him better I learned much that was plain common sporting sense. Jimmy did not strive for success. He just obtained it by the simple virtues of doing whatever he had to do in the correct way. With the ball he maintained that given a good length a bowler could not go far wrong. With the bat he argued and often demonstrated that runs must come if the bat was held straight and played straight. He also placed great faith in a good eye and one of his stern commands when, in his veteran days, he began to help out with coaching at the junior nets was to 'keep your eye on the ball all the time'. It paid off handsomely for him. On that memorable day when he captured all ten Oldham wickets he needed the help of only one fieldsman – the wicket-keeper – for eight of his victims were bowled and the other two caught behind. Year after year he gave Lionel Cranfield masterly support and between them the pair were good enough to trouble the best batsmen and bowlers in the league. Strangely enough Jimmy did not make a good captain. He was appointed for one season but begged to be relieved of the duties before the half-way stage. He was so wrapped up in his own individual effort he often forgot the needs of the side a as whole.

When he stood down another old-timer took over at Middleton. His name was Bob Murray and he had experienced a lot of cricket in the Lancashire League before taking up a business appointment in the town. He was an opening bat and a very shrewd judge of cricket and cricketers. He had a gruff manner and I was one of a bunch of youngsters in and out of the senior team at the time who

christened him 'Robert the Brute'. Yet his coaxing and even bully-
ing of us made the game easier to play and better to understand.
His sense of humour was keen but often misunderstood, especially
by those who only heard his gruff commands and comments. I
recall one match in which the opposing professional, a fastish
left-hander, was causing one of our younger set quite a lot of
trouble as he struggled to get established at the crease. The
skipper was at the other end and the youngster, in desperation,
went down to complain that the professional was throwing
instead of bowling. He was astounded to recieve a reprimand
instead of a consoling word for the skipper snapped back at him:
'Throwing? I know he is. . . but he's chucking so bloody badly
tha ought to be hitting him for six, not grousing.' Another
example of Bob Murray's shrewd reasoning centred around myself one sunny afternoon when, feeling on top of the world, I
hammered one untidy amateur bowler for four fours in an over.
The skipper came striding down the pitch to beckon me up for
what I thought would be a word of praise. Instead I got a roasting
for he said: 'What's tha playing at? If tha hits him for four more
fours they'll take him off. Use thi loaf and take one or two bound-
aries an over. . . we want him on, not off.'

Chapter 3

Heroes Off the Field, Too

Every league cricket club of my acquaintance had its men of stature, on and off the field. Government of a club is usually by a committee, variable in size but unshakeable in devotion to duty. The selection of the committee, an annual affair, was of great importance. Many maintained that choosing the off-the-field team was far more important than naming the one to play. The ideal committee blend was to get equal representation of workers and thinkers. Business men were needed to make the decisions, workmen to carry them out, and here again Middleton, always my yardstick in league cricket, were ideally served. Foremost amongst the men who got their coats off to produce results was my own father. He had never been a cricketer of more than Sunday School League standard but he loved the game with a passion that enabled him to make sacrifices so that I and my twin brother could play it at a better level than ever he achieved. In the record books of Central Lancashire League cricket it is easy to trace how and what Edwin and John Kay did for Middleton but only those who lived and worked with him at the time really knew what Teddy Kay achieved off-the-field. He was an engineer by trade and a tireless worker by instinct. If a job needed doing and the club funds would not permit labour to be engaged he would roll up his sleeves, rally round his friends, and produce the desired effect.

One long and cold winter he slaved four and five nights a week converting a heavy horse-pulled roller into a mechanical one. He and his labourers, and I counted myself one of them, went round the second-hand car scrap heaps until we found an old car engine that could be adapted for the purpose. It had to be stripped and rebuilt, mounted afresh and generally retuned and the task

represented something of an engineering miracle. But by dint of
much hard work and many hard words the transformation was
completed and when it came time for the job to be tested the odds
against the new-fangled machine sparking first time up were
tremendous. But it did and the cheers that came from an isolated
wind-swept garage one dark night late in February must have
startled quite a few passers-by. There was, however, one snag.
Something had gone wrong with the steering system in setting up
the new 'monster' and when my father in the driving seat turned
left the machine went right. Consternation? Not in league cricketing circles where necessity was often the mother of invention. The
hard way out was to strip it down and start again. The easy way
out was to paint a warning on the cab to make it quite clear to all
who drove that to turn left one had to steer right. With a new
season fast approaching this was the answer and the heaviest
roller I have ever seen stayed that way to do yeoman service for
more than thirty years before it finally went to the scrapheap
instead of a museum. It was, of course, often the butt of the local
paper cartoonist when it failed to start or got stuck in between
innings but by and large that roller was a symbol of the enthusiasm that makes league cricket what it is – a game played and
administered with blinding passion.

There was another major crisis at Middleton in the 1930s. The
fencing at one end of the ground had rotted beyond further repair
and the club committee, fearfully seeking tenders for replacement,
were also being urged to provide some covered accommodation for
the bigger crowds the team was then attracting. But money was
scarce and labour costs were mounting. Influential members of the
committee, the businessmen no less, used their influence without
avail. The lowest tender was for £500 and the sum was beyond
raising. In stepped the 'workers' on the committee. Seeking out
advice and aid from local builders they set about erecting their own
grandstand. Players and spectators were roped in for week-end
labour parties and in two months between Christmas and Easter a
wall and a roofed stand was built at the cost of materials only.
Even bricks and mortar were bought at scrap prices and although
there were rumours of dissatisfaction in the building union

quarters of the town nobody stepped in to prevent the job being completed or the labour force being depleted. Saturday afternoons and Sunday mornings saw thirty or so strong men working away under the supervision of one or two who had a smattering of experience in the building line.

When snags were struck, as frequently they were, a quiet word in the ear of a local building contractor who was a cricket fanatic, saw things sorted out and it was a mighty proud bunch of miscellaneous workers, among them were clerks, shopkeepers, schoolteachers and local publicans, who raised the sort of cheer that comes with the completion of a job well done. That stand is still in use today – and it is a monument to men behind league cricket. But there is not a league cricket club in the land that is not in need of money. It was always so. Undoubtedly it will ever be so. A club's main income comes from membership. Often the sum contributed annually is ridiculously low and there are many clubs today whose membership fees are very little 'up' on what they were twenty-five years ago when a pound went a lot farther than it does today.

Ideally a club should aim to budget its running costs against its income from membership – money guaranteed come sunshine or rain throughout the summer. But no club could live that way. Without exception there has always been a need for 'outside' efforts to raise the cash. Gate receipts, of course, are always unpredictable and winter after winter club committees, aided and abetted by their ladies' sections, have to devise ways and means of bringing in the extra money. In the old days a whist drive or a jumble sale would help tide things over but if there was a major outlay to be met a club bazaar or the old-fashioned sale of work was often the only answer. In later years there came the football 'buster' offering prizes for the highest number of goals over a certain period and demanding the selling of tickets – another labour of love for the hard-working committee members and their helpers. Nowadays it is still essential to boost the income from membership and gate receipts and again football, once cricket's biggest enemy, has been harnessed to help out financially and few clubs can manage without its weekly pools. The bigger clubs rely

1. Lionel Cranfield, Middleton professional who inspired a batch of promising youngsters.

2. Fred Duerr, one of the most successful amateur bowlers in the Lancashire League, and taker of more than 2000 wickets for Bacup and Ramsbottom.

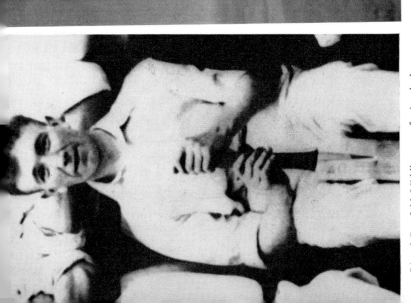

3. Billy Fenwick, the first amateur bowler to capture 100 wickets in a Lancashire League season. He played with Ramsbottom.

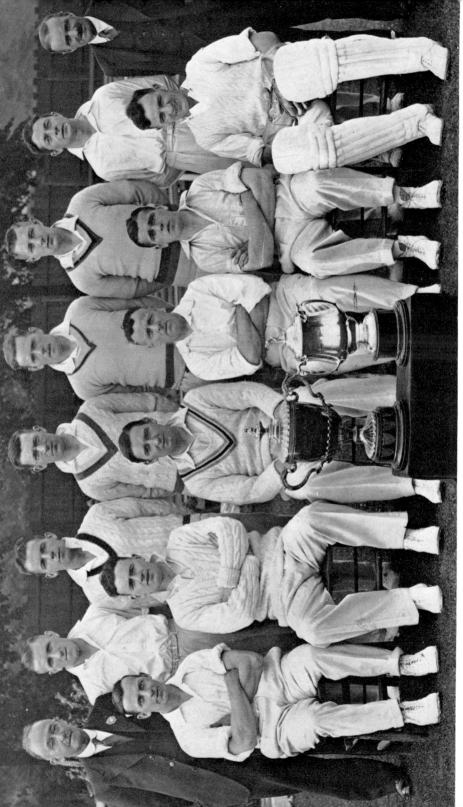

West Indies Team photograph prior to the World Cup in 1975. Leslie Warburton, the club professional

upon their bar and social activities out of season to meet the ever-rising costs, and whilst at one time it was essential for a cricket club to have a good social section it is now becoming fashionable for cricket to be just a section of a strong social club. It is a trend to be regretted for it undermines the very structure of cricket itself.

The question may well be asked if it is necessary to live so expensively in league cricket? Professionalism is indeed a costly business today and many leagues have forsaken it. There can be good cricket without professionals but the Lancashire League in particular and one or two others in the North of England, will not admit to this. In the old days £5 a week was a princely salary for a professional who also had to be a groundsman and the great Sydney Barnes once said that even in his hey-day he never got more than £10 a week – in golden sovereigns – as the reward for his work in the Lancashire or Central Lancashire Leagues. I doubt, too, if he ever got that much in the Staffordshire League. The trend to big-name professionals really began in the late 1920s when Nelson, the Lancashire League club who have a world-wide reputation for seeking out the best players in the world, persuaded Learie Constantine, the brightest star of an attractive West Indies touring team in England in 1928, to become their professional. Previously Nelson had astonished the cricketing world by en-gaging first-class cricketers of the calibre of Ted McDonald (Australia and Lancashire) and George Geary (England and Leicestershire) as their professional but the big 'breakthrough' came with the signing of Constantine in 1929.

'Connie', as everybody knew him, was the ideal league cricketer. His fast bowling was always a magnet for the crowd. His big hitting was an added attraction and his superlative fielding was a third factor in bringing to Saturday afternoon cricket in Lancashire a lustre that made both the Nelson club and the Lancashire League world famous. But Learie Constantine had other assets. He was in every sense of the word a gentleman. His standards on and off the field were as high as the ones he set at the wicket and with the ball. He dominated yet did not obliterate. He encouraged the amateurs he played alongside and praised them as fellow cricketers on the

c

same high level. He once said of Alf Pollard, an amateur bowler who shared the attack with him for years, that 'he never bowled a full toss or a long hop in ten years at Seedhill'. He probably overstated the virtues of a man who represented the perfect amateur cricketer but Learie Constantine counted himself fortunate he had such men as Pollard as colleagues and not opponents.

In 'Chick' Hawkwood he had a batting colleague he considered good enough to play for Lancashire and England and whom he eventually persuaded to take a chance with the county at Old Trafford although, alas, he never quite made the grade. Yet in his very first Lancashire-Yorkshire match Hawkwood hit a memorable century and always looked the kind of player who had the shots and the temperament to become a top-class cricketer. I do not know what 'Connie' thought of Hawkwood's inability to produce his best with Lancashire but it would not surprise me if he considered a delightful batsman lacked the right kind of encouragement once he got to county level. The Nelson team in Constantine's days attracted the biggest crowds ever to watch league cricket and when there was a hint that Rochdale were trying to tempt the West Indies all-rounder into the Central Lancashire League the rest of the Lancashire League clubs readily responded to a 'pool' to provide the money that kept Constantine in their midst to guarantee them a three-figure gate whenever he and Nelson were the visitors. The measure of the regard which Nelson, in particular, and the Lancashire League in general held for Constantine is best illustrated by the story of the schoolmaster who had not the heart to chastise pupils who answered an examination question asking 'Who was Constantine the Great?' by simply stating 'He was Nelson's professional'.

Such was fame for Learie Constantine a cricketer extra-ordinary who, in later years, went back 'home' to Nelson to receive the freedom of the town at a gathering unequalled for its emotional and sincere regard for a man and a cricketer. Now a man of high standing and deep learning Lord Constantine still has an abiding affection not only for Nelson but for its people and its memories. He went there with some trepidation, a coloured cricketer with a desire to please and a firm resolve not to let his race down. He did not. From his first day in the town to his last he was regarded as a perfect citizen and a magnificent cricketer. If the people of Nelson were good to Learie Constantine he can, although he probably never would, also maintain he was good for them. Mutual respect for one another grew into regard, even into love, and the legends created by Learie Constantine in Nelson and in Lancashire are not confined to cricket.

Nelson will never forget Constantine, the bowler who hurled himself into the fray with the fury of a tempest; the batsman who hit so hard the very willow broke; and the fieldsman who moved with lightning speed and electric effect. Truly the League Cricketer of All Time! His deeds were indeed mighty ones. But one does not need the record books to prove the greatness of 'Connie'. In essence Constantine put league cricket on the map and wherever he went he filled the grounds, some tiny, others large. Rarely did he fail to entertain with either bat or ball or in the field. Frequently he returned astounding figures with bat and ball but he also knew the meaning of the word failure for more than one local boy managed to dismiss him cheaply or hit him hard and in doing so illustrated the greatest charm of league cricket – the overthrowing of the mighty by the unknown. Whenever this happened there was no bitterness in the heart of Learie Constantine. He would go out of his way to pay tribute to the hero of the moment and admonish the greedy ones in the crowd who felt themselves deprived of a Saturday afternoon cricket feast. Behind the scenes, in the privacy of the dressing room, or the living room of many a Nelson cottage, there were stories told of Constantine's zest for lending a helping hand. No sick supporter ever lacked a pre-match word or even a hospital visit to provide the sort of medicine no doctor could better. Maybe he could not cure the ills of the flesh but when it came to boosting the spirits none did better work than Learie Constantine of Nelson, and the West Indies. And I do not think he will mind me placing Nelson first in order of importance.

Chapter 4

A Yorkshireman Takes Over

When Learie Constantine joined Nelson in 1929 there was another cricketer stepping into the league sphere with Middleton – and he came to make his mark rather than to supply experience or continue along the lines of Lionel Cranfield. His name was Hedley Verity and he came to Middleton from Accrington, the Lancashire League club, where he had struggled through a very ordinary season on branching out into Lancashire cricket after making steady progress with Rawdon and Horsforth, a couple of Yorkshire village sides which are so much part and parcel of the White Rose cricketing scene. Hedley Verity was a quiet and studious cricketer with a burning ambition to get to the top. He was 21 when he joined Accrington and it was his misfortune to find the club cluttered up with good players on the aging side. He was the club professional, yet the baby of the side, and it is no reflection upon either Accrington or Verity that neither club nor player made any great impact.

But at Middleton Verity found himself in a side in which at least six members were of his own age group. He also found a skipper in Ernest McDougall who was not only a good all-round cricketer and a keen student of the game, but a family man with two young sons, who years later, were to follow him and Verity into the Middleton side. It was a happy combination and yet, in the first season, there was little to hint of the glory ahead for Hedley Verity. He was tall and angular, a left-hand bowler who swung the ball into the right-handed batsmen and away from the left. He sometimes straightened it on pitching and usually managed to find an economical length. With the bat he was correct and not without scoring strokes and in the field he could hold his catches in the gully or race round the outfield should the occasion arise but very few people, in Middleton or elsewhere in the Central

Lancashire League, rated Verity more than a 'useful' all-round cricketer. They gained that impression from his performance in matches. We who were in the side with him knew him better. At the nets and in the dressing-room Hedley Verity set an ideal example.

He was shrewd enough to know that at the age of 21 he could not presume to go about his job of coaching and encouraging team spirit in the manner of a more experienced cricketer. He seldom asserted the authority that was his as the club professional unless all other means of persuading his fellow players had failed. He never once suggested things should be done his way. Yet he got us all to do what he wanted without question and without much argument. At the nets there was discipline. Smoking was frowned upon and fielding was important. It was not enough to bowl a spell and bat a spell. Each and every player, first, second or third-teamer, had to conform to a pattern and they readily did for the simple reason that Hedley Verity set the example. There were arguments, about field placings, about bowling changes, and even about the state of the wicket. The skipper held the reins but he was always prepared to accept a majority decision – on the field and off. It was Ernest McDougall's gift for understanding and Hedley Verity's appreciation of an ideal cricketing set-up that paved the way to his success with Yorkshire and with England.

In his first season, bowling seamers, although the term was not then in general use, Verity collected some 70 wickets at reasonable cost. With the bat he averaged in the low thirties and aggregated something like 600 runs and held the catches that came his way. There was no league title and no Wood Cup triumph for Middleton in 1929. But the way ahead was being clearly plannned and when, at the start of the 1930 season, Verity returned from his home at Rawdon to resume his job as the Middleton professional, things began to happen. Before the first match, and in the vital pre-season net practices, Verity had anounced that he was in future going to bowl spinners! He had been a regular attender at the Yorkshire indoor nets throughout the winter months and George Hirst, who must have had few peers as an all-round cricketer, had taken him aside to suggest that as a seamer he was one of many available to the county. As a spinner, if he concentrated on the job, he would have a better chance because Wilfred Rhodes was contemplating retirement.

Verity seized the opportunity. He never doubted his ability to produce what was required but it meant starting all over again and to do this he needed the co-operation of all with whom he played. He told his Middleton skipper all about it and was not only given the 'go ahead' but also a promise that everybody at Towncroft was behind him. Such was the team spirit that no questions were raised and no doubts cast when, in the first two or three games, Verity met with little bowling success. The Middleton committee, like the players, had every faith in their studious professional and they knew as well as did the team that the damp and cold of April and early May and the sodden pitches were of no help in a bold cricketing experiment. Patience was as essential as encouragement and in a few weeks' time the results began to appear. But it is necessary to go behind the scenes a little to find the true reason for Verity's successful change-over from seamer to spinner and from a good cricketer to an outstanding one. It was a question of environment.

In his first season Hedley, then a bachelor, had been found lodgings near the ground but with an old couple who had little or no interest in cricket. He was well fed and generally well looked after but he did not get enough of what he needed most – the cricket atmosphere. In 1930 he came to lodge with the Kays. Two sons in the side and a father on the committee, plus a mother who patiently understood the importance of the game, and a couple of sisters who often wondered what it was all about but never questioned the rightness of it all, set the scene for cricket, morning, noon and night. From April to September it was cricket for breakfast, cricket for lunch, cricket for tea and even more cricket for supper – and it was the supper sessions that were most important! Without fail, but not until the practice session had ended and the match pitch had been rolled, the Kay brothers and Hedley Verity would return home with three, four, sometimes five and six, members of the side, for a fish and chip supper and a debate on the current cricketing topic. Sometimes there would be a short break

with one of the boys on the piano for a few minutes but sooner
rather than later the cricket discussions began and they went on
until midnight or even later.

It did not need Verity to open the debate. It could be anybody –
and particularly one who had failed the previous match. He would
ask what we all thought about the manner of his dismissal and then
would come a searching cricketing analysis of a major or minor
problem. There would be differences of opinion. Quite often there
was no degree of unanimity about how the unlucky batsman got
out. He would, perhaps, lean to the view that the ball came in
quickly from the off. If the batsman at the other end at the time
was one of the party he would almost certainly disagree and even
those who only saw it from a distance, either the dressing-room
window or the vantage point behind the bowler's arm where the
late batsmen were prone to gather before it came their turn to bat,
would advance their personal theories. Sometimes it was a bowler,
and quite often the professional himself, who was the subject of
debate. Was he giving the ball too much air? Did he really need
two slips when the ball was not turning all that much? Was it wise
to dispense with extra-cover against opponents who batted without regard for the text book or the pitch or length of the ball?

These were cricketing questions debated at length and sometimes heatedly. Often there was no real solution but the discussions
were all part of a cricketing education that made the Middleton
team one to be feared. In 1930 the side were the Central Lancashire
League Champions and Wood Cup winners and in 1931 the Cup
was retained despite the frequent absence of Verity on duty for
Yorkshire. By then, he had made the break-through, and although
his contract with Middleton called for him to play in every match
he was never refused permission to take his chance with the county.
That was where the Middleton committee played as important a
part as did their players. They were men of understanding and
they had no desire nor intention to stand in Hedley Verity's way.
They had seen him work hard to earn his big chance. And they
were certainly not going to deny him it although it resulted in
Middleton losing several vital matches and with them the championship. It was their understanding, coupled with the support of

the players, and the encouragement of the supporters, members and casual watchers as well, that meant so much to Verity in his climb to the top. He appreciated their patience and their help – and never forgot either those he played with or those he worked for.

But there were problems and Verity had his share. His success with Middleton in 1930 and 1931 brought him offers to return to the Lancashire League at the sort of money that was regarded as 'big' in those days. He could have signed a three-year contract with one club and been a rich man by staying in league cricket. But he had set his eyes on playing for Yorkshire who, however, offered him no advice nor any security until he made the grade. It was the Yorkshire custom then, as it is today, not to give contracts. Certainly there was no guarantee of regular money or a place in the side until a man was awarded his county cap. And there was no easy way to a Yorkshire cap in the 1930s. Hedley Verity knew it. But he was prepared to throw away the substance of good money in the leagues for the shadow of fame and fortune that might come his way with Yorkshire. I recall him going to my father for advice. He had received a splendid offer from a Lancashire League club and they were pressing for an answer. His own father was away from home at the time and had not then replied to his son's letter seeking parental guidance. He had played for his county and done well. In the inner circle of Yorkshire cricket Herbert Sutcliffe, Maurice Leyland and Emmott Robinson were dropping hints that Verity was the one to succeed Wilfred Rhodes. But club officials said little – nay, they said nothing, and Verity was at the crossroads. He was engaged to be married and security was within his grasp. He knew what he wanted but had no assurance beyond his own confidence that he could attain his objective.

'What shall I do?' was the question he put to my father. 'What do you want to do?' was the immediate reply. Hedley Verity frankly and courageously admitted he had only one thought in his mind – to take his chance with Yorkshire. 'Then do so, but give it all you have got,' was my father's final advice. Down to the Post Office went a still bemused cricketer and he sent off a telegram declining the Lancashire League club's offer. The very next morning his father's letter arrived and it contained the same advice almost word for word. The rest is cricketing history. Hedley Verity went on to make a notable contribution to Yorkshire and England cricket until he met an early death in World War II.

In Middleton today there are old cricketers still around who proudly recall the tall, angular and grey-haired professional, who set them an example in cricket that could not be bettered. They quietly boast they played a small part in the grooming of a famous cricketer and if Hedley Verity were alive today he would be equally proud to admit it was a Lancashire club and Lancashire players who helped him most at the most critical period in his cricketing life. The days when he switched from swingers to spinners and earned for himself the chance to take over from Wilfred Rhodes.

Chapter 5

A Glorious Cricketing Era

Hedley Verity was one of the men who started league cricket in Lancashire off on a glorious decade in the 1930s. This is not my opinion alone but also that of many other old-timers that the Central Lancashire League as well as the Lancashire League and others up and down the country, was never stronger than in the years before World War II. Perhaps it can be traced to the coming of Learie Constantine. Certainly his magnificent all-round cricket led to an upsurge in crowd support and general interest that has never been bettered apart, perhaps, from the late 1940s. Certainly the 1930s were vivid years in my cricketing memories. There was not only an all-round strength, both professional and amateur, that made for good cricket but there was also better weather and few counter-attractions. To watch cricket on a Saturday afternoon was the aim of the sporting public generally. Most of them worked until lunchtime and travelling farther afield than the local cricket ground was a little out of the question. But what was the point of it so long as the league clubs up and down Lancashire provided the sort of entertainment that pleased? Constantine had with him in the Lancashire League such great players as Manny Martindale, George Headley and Edwin St Hill, and battling for supremacy with the West Indian stars were Australian fast bowler, Ted McDonald, Australian Test match all-rounder, Arthur Richardson and the former England bowlers George Macaulay and Fred Root. They made up a batch of formidable opponents for the amateurs but they seldom outshone them as did the overseas invasion that was to follow in the 1940s.

Constantine never tired of paying tribute to his amateur colleagues. In Chick Hawkwood and Clarrie Winlow he had batsmen who would be welcome in any county side today and with the ball few professionals ever had better support than that provided by the ageless Alf Pollard, the man who seldom bowled a long hop or a full toss and took wickets galore by simply, in his own quiet words, 'doing a bit either way off the pitch or in the air'. There in a nutshell was the recipe for good bowling. The Lancashire League matches were attracting crowds big enough to bring in gate receipts of over £300 when admission prices ranged from three-pence to one shilling and memberships were at their highest levels. Wherever Constantine and Nelson went you needed to be an early arrival to secure a seat and many an ardent cricket lover of that period has been content to stand for five hours to watch the local boys do battle with the world-famous professionals. Their joy was unconfined whenever the amateur outshone the paid player and it happened frequently although, alas, the Press, even then, was prone to give its headlines to the famous at the expense of the unknown.

The story was the same in the Central Lancashire League. It could be argued that the professionals were not quite of the same international quality but there were few better left-hand spinners than the West Indian, Ellis Achong, and no greater hitter of the ball than the New Zealander Ted Badcock, who was almost as big an attraction at Werneth as Constantine at Nelson. Yet, even if it had to yield pride of place in professionalism to the Lancashire League, the Central Lancashire League had in Leslie Warburton a pro-fessional equal to the best in any age and any sphere. A product of the Lancashire League club, Haslingden, where he owed a great deal to the patience and encouragement of Frank Edwards, Warburton was an all-round cricketer of rare talent. He began his professional career in the Saddleworth League before he was of age but his great days were spent with Littleborough who won the Central Lancashire League championship in 1932, 1934, 1935 and 1936 and also captured the Wood Cup in the 1935 season.

Warburton, outstanding wherever he played was a fast bowler and early-order batsman whom Lancashire coveted greatly but could not persuade into first-class cricket apart from occasional games against Yorkshire, and a Test trial at Lords. Modest though his returns with bat and ball were in first-class cricket he left no doubts about his ability at the highest level and quickened Lancashire's determination to woo him away from the Saturday afternoon game. It was the perfect example of from village green to Test match scene but Warburton still refused to leave the security of a steady banking job for the insecurity of first-class cricket with his native county. It has been said that Tommy Higson, the Lancashire official who was then a Test selector, 'engineered' Warburton's appearance at Lord's in an endeavour to impress a cricketing youngster with the majesty and power of the game at the highest level. Be that as it may Leslie Warburton remained a league cricketer all his playing days.

He had, of course, the advantage of playing with a team of talented amateurs. The Littleborough skipper of those days was Harry Butterworth, a Cambridge Blue and an amateur all-rounder always welcomed in the Lancashire county side when he could spare time from the family business of baking bread and cakes to appear at Old Trafford or elsewhere. Harry Butterworth was not only an attractive batsman and a clever leg-spinner, he was also a fine fieldsman. But his greatest gift was of being a leader. He gathered round him a team of Littleborough boys, some of whom worked for Butterworth as well as played for him and they made up one of the strongest league sides I ever saw or played against. With the new ball Warburton was a deadly attacker. He had pace far above the average for a league player and with it he combined ability to swing the ball either way and occasionally make it 'wobble' in the air. He was a strong fellow who could bowl for a long spell without losing pace or direction and in all with Littleborough he captured well over 600 wickets in five glorious seasons. He was fortunate, and never failed to admit this, in having an opening partner who was as good as any amateur bowler league cricket has produced. Tommy Gilfoy was not a Lancashire man. He came from the North-east but he lived, worked and played at Littleborough throughout the 1930s and was the ideal foil for Warburton's often blistering pace. He bowled at medium pace and swung the ball just a little either way. His greatest asset, however, was his talent for keeping the perfect length and the ideal direction. You were a lucky batsman indeed if you could pad up and let a Gilfoy delivery go by without making a shot.

Warburton and Gilfoy made a formidable pair of opening bowlers and to follow Littleborough had, if they needed it, the spin of Butterworth and the cutters of Sammy Southwell, a cricketer who could never fail to entertain because he was superb in the field and a big hitter with the bat. If runs were wanted in a hurry Sammy was the man for the job and in Harry Johnson and Phil Mitchell, Littleborough also had two batsmen capable of getting runs in the best of league cricketing company. A happy side, led by a shrewd and inspiring captain, Littleborough were one of the strongest league sides of all time, for in addition to having the men who could get runs and take wickets they were also brilliant in the field. Their strength grew under the careful grooming of that dour but delightful Yorkshireman, Emmott Robinson, who was professional for two years before Warburton took over and concentrated upon building for the future. Emmott did a magnificent job with Littleborough. He joined the club when the team was creaking with middle age but settled down to discover and encourage the next generation of players. It was once said to Emmott, just before he left the delightful Little-borough ground at Hare Hill, that the club had not won any cups under his guidance. Shrewdly, and with a touch of Yorkshire spirit, Robinson replied: 'Cups? Nay, ah've had to do too much sorting out. But dunna fret, mantlepiece'll be full this next year or two.' How right he was.

The major threat to Littleborough in the Central Lancashire League battles of the 1930s usually came from Rochdale, Werneth or Middleton and there was another talented batch of young amateur players at Werneth under Ted Badcock. A mighty hitter with the bat and a medium-paced seamer who turned to off-spinners when the ball lost its shine, Badcock's fielding was top-class and he helped marshal Werneth into a fine side. They had an opening pair of batsmen in Harry Potter and Jack Plant who could master the best bowlers in the league and coming in at No. 3 was Clifford Stott, a stylist and a run-scorer, who would have been welcome at Old Trafford had he not, like Leslie Warburton, preferred the security of a bank to the uncertainty of first-class cricket. Stott played in glasses but they were no handicap. He scored centuries or half centuries on every Central Lancashire League ground and could also be relied upon to bowl several economical overs if required. In the field he had a safe pair of hands and uncanny anticipation when fielding close to the wicket. I know. He frequently aided and abetted in my dismissal season after season. But there were others beside Potter, Plant and Stott, to render vital aid to Badcock. Arnold Hilton was a delightful batsman to watch and Bill Lawton, who later married the stage star Dora Bryan and played a couple of games for Lancashire in between taking professional posts in various leagues, was a steady and sometimes destructive off-spinner. For the 'funny' stuff, leg-breaks, off-breaks and googlies, Werneth had Jimmy Olsen who tossed the ball high in the air and baffled batsman after batsman by the very simplicity of his command over length and turn.

Rochdale always had a top-notch professional and in Ellis Achong they had a left-hander who was seldom collared. He was, perhaps, not quite so well supported as Warburton at Littleborough or Badcock at Werneth, but in Eric Silverwood he had a batting stylist and in Sammy Barlow a sound defensive and by no means unattractive opening batsman. Middleton slumped a little after Hedley Verity had gone. Never a wealthy club it could not branch out into the international field for its professional but when Verity went some good players had spells at Towncroft. Horace Fisher was one. This talented Yorkshire left-hander had full reason to bemoan his cricketing fate. If Yorkshire requested Verity's release from Middleton duty it was part of the bargain that the county provided a substitute professional – and the choice always fell upon Fisher. Horace was, at that time, a Yorkshire colt allocated to the Barnsley club, and he was a fine cricketer, batting left-handed and possessing a wide range of scoring strokes, and bowling left-handed either seam or spin. He used to come to Middleton with a justified cricketing chip on his shoulder for if Verity's release had been refused – it never was – Fisher would have gone into the Yorkshire side. He maintained that he got 'mucky end o' stick' and was aggrieved.

But it did not affect his cricket or his performance although it did, undoubtedly, limit his first-class career to a very short span just before World War II. He eventually signed for Middleton after a hard battle over terms finally concluded by an agreement that for every wicket he took over 100 he would get an extra pound. By early August Fisher had reached the three figure stage and I was the first to drop a catch that would have brought him an extra pound. I apologized and was told: 'It's aw reet, give me ten bob and I'll call it square.' Horace Fisher was undoubtedly the only Middleton professional who ever demanded his wages in cash before the start of every game. He used to stuff ten one pound notes down his knee length white stockings before he took the field and never trusted a bank or a cheque book.

I make no apologies for singing the merits of the Middleton amateur strength of those days. Nor do I hesitate to nominate my twin brother, Edwin, as one of the best batsmen in the history of the club. He played for Middleton for 25 years, scored well over 10,000 runs, hit nearly a half century of centuries and skippered the side for years. His ability to play forward or backward with equal application earned him a reputation second to none in Central Lancashire League circles and for a brief spell I opened the innings with him – a pairing forced upon the skipper in our early days because one or two umpires took a poor view of Edwin opening the innings and getting quite a few runs and then, until they finally saw us together, confusing them by coming back for what they thought was a second knock. We were not as alike as two peas but we were sufficiently similar to cause confusion and concern. It was an amicable solution to send us both in together, Edwin wearing a cap and me going without one, and we had our good times together to give the side a good start and once earned praise from the late Donny Davies who, writing on league cricket for the then '*Manchester Guardian*', described us as 'the Sutcliffe and Holmes of league cricket'. It was high praise, especially for Edwin who was, of course, the Sutcliffe and the stylist. But we were not alone. Leslie Sigsworth was a fine all-rounder and Tom Jacques a superb off-spinner – a bowler with as perfect an action as any I saw. We had, too, an impish wicket-keeper by the name of Freddie Pearson whom Hedley Verity regarded as one of the best who ever kept to him – and said so after years in first-class cricket.

Chapter 6

Youth was Given its Fling

In the 1930s Middleton sent several good young players to Old Trafford. That few of them made the grade was more a reflection upon Lancashire's system of coaching than on any false pretentions at Middleton – Jack Wilson, Monty Cranfield, Ernest Steele, Cliff Cooke and Stan Proffitt were the equal of many a county cricketer today. From the point of view of providing players or a stepping stone to bigger things this little Middleton club has quite a reputation. Hedley Verity started the trend. Later came Eric Price, of Lancashire and Essex, and Frank Tyson in whom Lancashire saw no promise. And what about Basil D'Oliveira? Middleton played an important part in his rise to cricketing fame.

Price was a local boy who came to the forefront the usual league cricket way. He was a keen and enthusiastic young left-hand spinner when at school and upon leaving he migrated to the town club where he spent hours at the junior nets, amusing himself most of the time but gradually coming under the wing of the club professional of the time. First it was Horace Fisher and then burly Steve Preston, a product of the Heywood Club who had joined the Old Trafford ground staff but never made the grade and returned to league cricket as a professional. He served Middleton well for three years, scoring runs at a fair pace and in attractive manner and grabbing his fair share of the wickets by bowling fast and medium in turn and generally doing a satisfactory job for a fair rate of pay.

When he moved on George Hargreaves took over and began at once to press the claims of young Price. Hargreaves was that rare league cricket asset – a sound player and a good club man. He had played league cricket in various spheres after serving his apprenticeship as an amateur with Enfield in the Lancashire

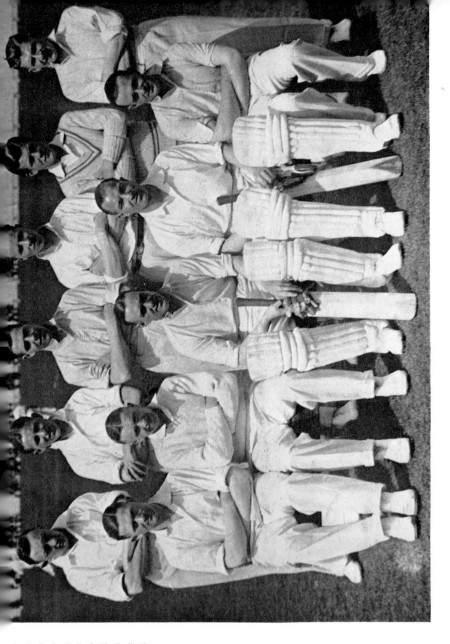

5. A picture of the Middleton team that won the Central Lancashire League championship and the Wood Cup in 1938. Eric Denison, the club's Yorkshire professional is seated second from the right in the front row between the Kay brothers, Edwin (with bat) and John.

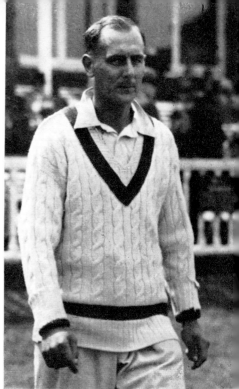

6. Alderman John Henry Wood, the Grand Old Man of Central Lancashire League cricket.

7. Hedley Verity, went from Middleton to play for Yorkshire and for England.

8. Sydney Barnes, the most devastating of all League bowlers.

League and he came to Middleton to bowl his leg-breaks with some success and get among the runs when they were most needed. George Hargreaves was not one of Middleton's most successful professionals, but he was one of the best liked because he never stopped trying. It was typical of Hargreaves that given the ball one sunny Saturday afternoon with the opposition sitting pretty needing some 20 or 30 runs to win with six or seven wickets in hand he would produce a deadly spell that brought victory against the odds. He was that sort of cricketer. If six wickets were needed with only six balls to bowl he would pronounce to the skipper or the opposition that 'we can just do it if we get stuck in'. It was in this sort of cricketing environment that Price made his Central Lancashire League debut and progressed slowly but surely to the stage when Lancashire started to show an interest.

Eventually he was persuaded to join the county staff at a wage of £3 a week for the summer only that looked and was meagre enough to deter all but the highly ambitious. As usual in those days there was much hard work to be done at the nets at Old Trafford and for two seasons young Price got nothing but net bowling and club and ground games. Then, in 1939, he forced his way into the county second eleven and was fast making a name for himself as a left-hand spinner of the future when war broke out; but when cricket at top level was resumed he returned to Old Trafford and soon forced his way into the Lancashire side despite the success of the longer established W. B. (Bill) Roberts. For a time Lancashire found room for two left-handers but Price lacked opportunity after appearing in an England trial at Canterbury in 1946 and he decided his future lay elsewhere.

He went to Essex but never really settled down in the South of England and returned North to play professionally in various leagues and eventually to make his way back to Middleton, this time as the club professional. And it was in this capacity that he tasted the real 'raw meat' of league cricket. One week he went out to capture all ten Littleborough wickets for a mere song, the next, he was on the receiving end as Radcliffe's opening pair, Frankie Worrell and Billy Greenhalgh, ran up a club and league record by scoring over 300 runs without being parted in a little

D

LITTLEBORO' V. MIDDLETON   26.4.52

MIDDLETON

E. Kay, c Nayudu, b Maden	34
J. M. Hyde, b Maden	34
J. Sharpe, b Gilfoy	1
H. McDougall, run out	6
J. Fisher, c Butterworth, b Maden	15
R. McDougall, c Maden, b Gilfoy	1
R. H. Partington, c Jackson, b Maden	3
F. Heywood, b Maden	2
K. Collinge, c Maden, b Taylor	24
W. Lee, not out	6
E. Price, c Blacklock, b Gilfoy	0
	128 all out

BOWLING	O.	M.	R.	W.	No balls
T. Gilfoy	18.7	7	37	3	2
S. Southwell	5	1	16	—	
C. S. Nayudu	2	—	21	—	
A. Maden	9	—	49	5	
D. Taylor	3	1	3	1	

LITTLEBORO'

R. Hawkard, c Partington, b Price	1
R. Jackson, b Price	8
J. Blacklock, lbw, b Price	0
S. Southwell, c Collinge, b Price	1
R. Whatmough, c Partington, b Price	2
C. S. Nayudu, b Price	13
J. Bowden, c Sharpe, b Price	0
S. Butterworth, b Price	3
D. Taylor, not out	0
A. Maden, b Price	0
T. Gilfoy, lbw, b Price	0
	31

BOWLING	O.	M.	R.	W.
K. Collinge	6	—	19	—
E. Price	8.7	5	4	10
J. Fisher	3	1	5	—

Two scorecards that dramatise the glorious uncertainty of cricket. One week Eric Price took all ten Littleborough wickets for four runs to set up a Central Lancashire League record. A few weeks later he was on the receiving end when Frank Worrell and Billy Greenhalgh set up another record for a first wicket partnership.

MIDDLETON V. RADCLIFFE   31.5.52

RADCLIFFE

F M Worrell not out				152
W Greenhalgh not out				144
Extras				7
Total (for 0 dec.)				303

Bowling:

E J Price	20	2	95	0
J A Fisher	11	0	51	0
K Collinge	10	3	73	0
H McDougall	7	0	52	0
J Sharpe	1	0	20	0
J M Hyde	1	0	5	0

MIDDLETON

J M Hyde st Hoyle b Olive	2
R McDougall not out	7
J Sharpe not out	4
Extras	1
Total (for 1)	14

Bowling:

F M Worrell	4.6	1	8	0	
J Olive	4	1	5	1	Match Drawn

over 2½ hours. But Middleton were not alone in providing Lancashire with good recruits. There was a steady supply from both the Central Lancashire and the Lancashire leagues but few really won through to make a success of first-class cricket. The reasons for their failure were many and varied but it could not be blamed on a lack of opportunity in the Saturday afternoon sphere as was the case after the war when professionalism ran riot and the world was scoured for men to fill the role of club professionals.

In the 1930s, for me the Golden Era of league cricket, there were many big-name professionals; but there were also many modest ones, both from the salary and the performance point of view, and it was these 'bread and butter professionals' who were the real heroes of league cricket at that time. Week after week there would be a train leaving Leeds soon after eleven o'clock on a Saturday morning that could aptly have been termed a cricketers' special. It picked up at such places as Bingley, Pudsey, Bradford and Halifax and brought over the border a batch of men who were good enough to satisfy the demands of the Lancashire league clubs who lived in the shadow of the Constantines, the Martindales and the Headleys.

There were right-hand fast bowlers and left-hand swingers. Off-break bowlers and left-hand spinners. Big hitting batsmen and dour defensive ones. They all played their part in the world that was league cricket before the second World War. Arthur Booth was one. He was one of many Yorkshire left-handers who could not hope to break into the county side so long as Hedley Verity played. So he settled for profitable Saturday afternoon professionalism. Billy Newton, a man who bowled fast and earnestly and slashed around happily with the bat until he was turned sixty, was another. There was little Fred Slater from Yeadon who had several golden years at Heywood, where his left-handed seamers accounted for batsmen galore and his stubborn batting saved or won many a game for a variety of clubs. There were the Claughton brothers, also from Yeadon, Alan and Hugh. And Squire Render, a giant of a man who used to bowl flat out for hours on end for Werneth and slogged his way happily to many a half-century that meant victory for his club and a collection for himself.

These, and so many others like them, did not ask for much money. Content with a wage, in the region of £5 a match, they augmented it by taking wickets and scoring runs to pick up talent money and collections – and they earned every penny they took home the hard way. The amateurs, too, accepted collections and in doing so heaped upon themselves much criticism from those who did not know league cricket well enough to realize that when the hat went round in appreciation of a good innings or a match-winning bowling return not all the proceeds went to the man who had done the deed. Almost without exception the amateurs in league cricket in the 1930s pooled their collections and used the cash to have a day out at the end of the summer, provide tackle for those who could not afford to buy their own, and generally smooth out the financial problems that arose from time to time.

If a player was off work through illness or injury it was not uncommon to help out with a pound or two in lieu of missing wages and I even recollect a collection pool being raided to pay the fine of a hard-hitting batsman who had celebrated neither well nor wisely after one glorious cricketing encounter and needed bailing out from the local police station. Great days, yes, and great players!

Chapter 7

Cricket under a Shadow

It was inevitable that league cricket in 1939 should be played under a shadow. Sportsmen everywhere were conscious of the possibility of war, but the cricket programme was almost complete before war eventually broke out. In Lancashire, Church were the team that mattered in the Lancashire League and in the Central Lancashire sphere the powerful Werneth side took the championship and Milnrow were the Wood Cup winners. Church took the Lancashire League championship and owed a great deal to the bowling of an amateur, Tommy Lowe, who captured 101 wickets at a cost of only 8.40 runs each, and later embarked upon a career of professionalism in several minor leagues as well as producing match-winning returns for several clubs in war-time cricket when professionalism was not recognized by the major leagues in the county.

There were, especially in the Central Lancashire League, many charges of sham amateurism but no direct evidence to prove the complaints justified. Yet it was a fact payment was being made by individual club members to the many professionals working in sheltered occupations or serving in the Armed Forces and stationed in Lancashire. It was inevitable that qualification restrictions, always stricter in the Lancashire League than the Central Lancashire League, would have to be waived to allow clubs to continue fielding two teams each summer week-end but by and large the Lancashire League stuck closer to their ideals than did their near neighbours and it was a frequent occurrence to see former first-class cricketers and league professionals appearing in the Central Lancashire League and doing much to keep the cricketing flag flying. Crowds, of course, were much smaller but there was still a public for league cricket as a relief and relaxation from the worries and trials of war.

There was also no lack of Sunday games in support of war charities and with both the Army and the Royal Air Force authorities understanding the need to keep cricket alive and the public entertained, many first-class players were allowed to take week-end leave. Championships and Cup successes were not of any great importance, but with Old Trafford blitzed and deserted for five whole seasons the leagues of Lancashire played a tremendous part in maintaining the game at an organized level.

There was no lack of personalities in the matches. Any cricketer of repute who happened to find himself stationed in or around Lancashire in war-time usually found an outlet for his skill at week-ends and I recall playing for Middleton in one Central League clash against a Crompton side that included nine cricketers with pre-war experience at first-class level. Charlie Hallows (Lancashire and England) opened the innings with Jack Cutmore (Essex) and coming in first wicket down was Norman Oldfield, who like Hallows, had played for Lancashire and England. Later in the batting order came Eddie Cooper, of Worcestershire, one of the many fine cricketers the Bacup club had provided for first-class counties, and following on was Learie Constantine who did a great war-time job as welfare officer among the many West Indians based on Merseyside.

Edwin St Hill, one of Constantine's colleagues in the West Indies touring side in the early 1930s, was also playing after serving as a professional in several of the leagues before war broke out. Jack Iddon, the stylish Lancashire left-hander, so unhappily killed in a road accident just before first-class cricket re-opened in 1946, was also a member of the side and so, too, were his county colleagues, Dick Pollard and Albert Nutter, and the Crompton side was completed by the inclusion of leg-spinner Jack Stopford, a member of the Old Trafford staff in 1939, and wicket-keeper Bernard Halley, the only local in the team and captain for the day.

Yet Crompton, with all their powerful 'guest' players, were beaten as often as they were victorious in those treasured cricketing days of World War II. One might well ask, indeed many did, how it came about that any one club should be in a position to turn out what amounted almost to an international test side when professionalism was barred for the duration. The question was always uppermost in the minds of the Central Lancashire League authorities and committee meetings were often the scenes of stormy debate with allegations in plenty but proof of payment completely absent. What was going on? The answer was simple. Clubs officially abided by the war-time rules to restrict cricket to an amateur sport but influential and wealthy club supporters often dipped into their own pockets to pay the 'expenses' of the stars – and there was little the League Committee could do about it.

In the words of one of their most prominent officials, Eli Bottomley, of the Oldham club, and a veritable John Bull in appearance and outspokenness, 'it was a fishy business and it certainly made you think!' But Bottomley, and his colleagues, knew that the appearance of the top-class players brought not only lustre but money to the clubs and the league for Constantine was still a crowd-puller and his many first-class colleagues and opponents proved equally attractive entertainers in the only cricketing medium left open to them. It might have been better had the Central Lancashire League been as open as was the Bradford League where professionalism thrived throughout two world wars and fees were very reasonable indeed. But be that as it may if some officials had troubled consciences others revelled in the appearance of the stars and it was also pleasing to observe that former league professionals were also willing and eager to appear as regularly as duties would permit, including such cricketers as Jack Holroyd, one of the most deadly left-hand spinners the leagues had produced between the two World Wars, Fred Slater and Ted Badcock, who, incidentally, played a prominent part in the blitz that hit Manchester and Salford when, as a leading member of the Auxiliary Fire Service, he earned distinguished mention for bravery under fire and was presented to the King and Queen when they paid a sympathetic visit to the city.

Travelling during war-time was always a major problem. Petrol was rationed and public transport severely restricted but somehow or other the league cricket public and players managed to get by. It was no uncommon thing for players to travel from home to ground, often quite a distance, by bicycle and I well recall one Middleton 'character' cycling to Royton to hit a half-century, grab a collection and cycle back home with cricket bag considerably heavier because of copper and silver coins to the amount of some five pounds.

They were strange days and memorable ones. It was not always possible to give either pitches or outfields the sort of attention regarded as necessary in peace time and it was not unusual to see both players and officials busy with cutter and roller almost up to starting time. Another aspect of war-time league cricket was the willingness of those who stayed at home and were able to play with some degree of regularity to stand down and allow their former colleagues a game whenever they were home on leave or could snatch a few hours off duty.

Proudly both the Lancashire and the Central Lancashire Leagues maintained cricket throughout the war years – something they had not been able to do in World War I when the Lancashire League closed down in 1917 and 1918 and their neighbours played only occasional games. There was, of course, a marked lack of publicity for league cricket in the war years and many a brilliant match-winning performance went unreported although the 'local rags' never failed to print scores and highlight the leading performances. But for the world at large cricket was at a standstill until 1945 when an opportunity was taken, with the end of hostilities in Europe, to re-introduce first-class cricket with a series of Victory Tests against an Australian Services side that contained many first-class players several of whom returned to this country to brighten up the league scene and set the scene for an unprecedented search around the world for the cricketers who were to make the 1950s the 'boom' days of league cricket.

In 1939 Accrington had done their best to tempt Don Bradman into Lancashire League cricket and tread in the footsteps of an earlier Australian cricketing generation represented by Ted McDonald who played with Nelson and Bacup and Arthur Richardson of Burnley and Bacup renown. If Accrington failed to lure Bradman to this country it was a failure that did not deter the Lancashire league clubs once the war was over and the leading players of the Australian Services side under Lindsay Hassett were a natural target for clubs anxious to resume on the most enterprising of cricket notes.

Rawtenstall proudly announced they had secured the signature of the man they, and the rest of the cricketing world, regarded as the brightest star of all. His name was Keith Miller but, alas, somewhere along the line something went wrong and Miller did not grace Lancashire League cricket, either with Rawtenstall or with any other club. He was just about the best cricketer who failed to succumb to the lure of league cricket but he sent over, to fill his place at Rawtenstall, a young New South Wales all-rounder who stayed on and on and on in England to play for Lancashire and then return to league cricket after also making a name for himself in League football over here. The youngster who stepped in for Keith Miller was Ken Grieves. But if Miller, like Bradman, remained out of reach the other Australian stars did not. Cec Pepper, always a controversial cricketing figure, joined Rochdale and then went on to Burnley and stayed in the leagues for fifteen years before he became a first-class umpire.

At his best Pepper must have been one of the most devastating of spin bowlers. His speed off the pitch was almost the equal of medium pace and his ability to turn the ball both ways and mix these highly talented skills with a baffling top-spinner made Pepper a sure 'winner' in league cricket parlance. Yet his bowling was only part of his cricketing armament. With the bat he was one of the biggest hitters I have ever seen and there are plenty of Scarborough Festival regulars who still talk about the day he drove several deliveries into the distant Trafalgar Square – hits that made Pepper world famous for in the course of the telling of the story it became a legend in India at least that Pepper once hit the ball so hard at Lord's it fell in Trafalgar Square. I once listened to an Indian old-timer telling this story in the lounge of one of Bombay's biggest hotels. Cricket loses nothing by this slight bending of the facts as Sir Neville Cardus would no doubt agree.

Pepper earned a reputation for being a firebrand both on and off the field. It is true the Australian had a colourful command of language and was wont to express himself in no uncertain terms to officials, to players and also to umpires. It was this indulgence in 'free speech' that led to Pepper upsetting several leading officials in Australian cricketing circles but their loss was the Lancashire league's gain and for years he attracted the crowds in the manner of Constantine and even outshining him by the power and regularity of his match-winning returns. Pepper helped to build a magnificent Rochdale side. He was the mainspring in the team that won the Central Lancashire League championship in 1948 and when he moved on to Burnley he produced the same brand of cricketing fireworks for the benefit of the Lancashire League public. His meritorious performances were legion, far too many to list, but let it suffice to tell that in his one season at Rochdale, back in 1948, he became the first overseas professional ever to hit more than 1,000 runs and take 100 wickets, a feat previously performed by Leslie Warburton at Littleborough before the second World War.

Pepper's returns with bat and ball in his 'high summer' in Central Lancashire League cricket were 1,083 runs and 102 wickets and these were the sort of figures he produced regularly in his hey-day as a league cricketer. Yet there were men who regarded Pepper as a bad influence on the Saturday afternoon game. They cited his frequent brushes with authority and recalled that umpires were being subject to more than their fair share of abuse. It was true Pepper often spoke out of turn, but he seldom meant any harm. His bark was certainly much worse than his bite and although he made enemies on and off the field he remained a great cricketer and a much sought-after professional. I knew him well in his Rochdale days and in my capacity as honorary secretary of the Central Lancashire League had at times to take him to task. In doing so I came to understand that whatever Pepper said in the heat of the cricketing moment was seldom meant and that he loved nothing better than to be answered back in the same colourful and lurid terms that he himself indulged in.

When this happened, and it frequently did, the air was cleared and all parties got on with the game. When umpires and officials took offence and reported the Australian it often meant an enquiry and a sentence but it was always plain to those who sat in judgment that Cec Pepper had far more goodness than badness in his soul. Certainly he got the headlines for his tantrums but seldom did he get the praise that was his due when he captured wickets, hit runs by the hundred, and in between doing so often put his hand in his pocket to buy equipment for many a hard-up amateur short of cricketing boots or flannels. A fool to himself? Maybe. But Pepper certainly deserved a better cricketing deal both in Australia and in England.

It was inevitable that he developed aspirations to sample county cricket in this country and he enlisted my aid to get in touch with a southern county. It was planned he should meet this county's secretary who was also the club captain when the southern side came north to meet Lancashire at Old Trafford. The meeting duly took place in a Manchester hotel and over a cup of tea and a very friendly discussion agreement was reached that Pepper's terms and conditions for a special registration should be placed before the southern county's committee. The discussion over, Pepper and I were walking out of the hotel with the visiting skipper when we bumped into a leading official of the Lancashire club. He beckoned the visitor aside and Pepper and I went on our way. The next morning upon enquiring of the visiting skipper about Pepper's prospect of engagement I was told, somewhat sorrow-fully: 'I am sorry but I have been hearing things about Pepper that make it impossible to continue with the negotiations.' And that was the end of the Australian's chances of breaking into top-class cricket in this country, until, years later, he was accepted as a first-class umpire. He had been condemned out of hand by a man who had heard the stories circulated about the New South Wales man's outspokenness but had no actual evidence of their accuracy or otherwise. This was the cross that Pepper had to bear most of his cricketing life. The many good things he did seldom gained publicity but whenever he transgressed he hit the headlines and suffered, even more, from the usual stretching of the facts by people who heard the stories at a distance and passed them on with added spice.

Chapter 8

The Australian Invasion

Pepper was the first of the talented post-war Australians who brought lustre to the Lancashire leagues. Close upon him came men like George Tribe, a left-hand spinner from Victoria who came to this country to join Milnrow and then, before moving on to first-class cricket with Northamptonshire, played for Rawtenstall and bamboozled batsmen by the sort of wrist spinning few English bowlers, Johnny Wardle excepted, tend to specialize in. Jock Livingston was another shrewd and attractive cricketer – a wicket-keeper-batsman who, unable to win a place in the powerful New South Wales side of those days, came to England to join Royton and put forth new and sound methods for coaching as well as playing. It is said, often with complete disregard for the facts, that Australian cricketers are a mercenary breed. Yet many of the Australians who came to Lancashire had much more to offer than attractive cricket and Livingston set about organizing coaching at Royton in a manner seldom before attempted or even contemplated.

He considered it his job not only to do well in the middle but also to produce and encourage the cricketers of the future and he made one impassioned plea to both his own club committee and to the League Committee in general to be allowed to play, and preferably skipper, the third team at Royton. It was an unprecedented approach and it was turned down without a thought of what lay behind it and what could spring from it. Livingston wanted to take net coaching a step further. It was his belief he could do a great deal better if he were on hand in the middle to direct operations in a teen-age side and advise and encourage in arts of strategy as well as scoring runs, taking wickets and holding catches. It was sound cricketing logic but the committee considered the Australian was pulling a fast one and wanted still more opportunities to produce figures in the middle. It was nothing of the kind. Livingston was thinking of the good he could do purely from a coaching point of view but his appeal fell on stony ground and not only Royton but the whole of league cricket suffered from this misinterpretation of a fine cricketer's blueprint for the future. Livingston, like Tribe, eventually joined Northamptonshire and contributed much to the first-class cricket scene in the midlands. Even today he is still around and playing most of his cricket with and against school sides – doing an immense amount of good in the manner that was scorned in Lancashire.

Sid Barnes – the New South Wales all-rounder, not the famous English bowler – was another league cricket recruit from Australia but his stay was brief although colourful. Barnes, one of cricket's greatest 'characters', joined Burnley for a time but never really settled down to the simple way of life so prevalent in a Lancashire cotton town. I really think Sid came into Lancashire League cricket believing he could make a fortune on and off the field. He stayed long enough to gather in plenty of runs and quite a few wickets but he told the story of his own disillusionment in a characteristic manner when he related his first experience of earning a league cricket collection. He scored his runs quickly and attractively in partnership with a local boy at the other end but when the hat went round the amateur received a far higher reward than the professional. This puzzled Sid and he asked an old-timer why it should be so.

He was told: 'It sarves thi reet. Tha turns up in a posh car and a flash suit. T'other fellow came on t' bus carrying his bag and wearing a shabby old suit. Folks round here notice these things.' The message went home. The very next match Barnes arrived by bus and was poorly dressed – but it was too late and his collections were always on the meagre side. Barnes soon travelled on but the Australians continued to arrive on the Lancashire league cricket scene and almost without fail they proved highly attractive professionals. Men like Bill Alley (Colne and Blackpool), Fred Freer (Rishton), Jack Pettiford (Nelson), Des Fothergill (Enfield), Jack Manning (Colne), Ken Archer (Accrington), Colin McCool

(East Lancashire), Bobby Simpson (Accrington), Ray Lindwall (Nelson), and Bruce Dooland (East Lancashire) set standards of the highest cricketing value and they made the Lancashire and Central Lancashire leagues the Mecca for the greatest players in the world.

The West Indies had started their own 'invasion' before the war with Learie Constantine, Manny Martindale, George Headley and Ellis Achong; but even their lustre paled into insignificance when, around 1951, the next generation of West Indians came over to shatter all records and build up attendance figures to phenomenal proportions. Frankie Worrell, Sonny Ramadhin, Alf Valentine, Clyde Walcott and Everton Weekes had provided the backbone of John Goddard's powerful touring team that conquered England in the summer of 1950 and they were natural targets for the enterprising league clubs ever seeking new faces. Most of them went to the Lancashire League but Worrell re-joined Radcliffe and Ramadhin went to Crompton to keep the Central Lancashire League in the picture and, let it be said without fear of contradiction, that when they arrived the cricket was never better. Worrell had sampled cricket at Radcliffe before touring with Goddard and he never ceased to sing the praises of league cricket to his colleagues. The West Indians had no opportunity to branch out professionally at home and the league clubs reaped a rich harvest, for without exception they were successful cricketers in the Saturday afternoon sphere. Their deeds are sprinkled liberally among the league records but each in turn suffered failure as well as enjoying success and there is no story that better illustrates the uncertainty of league cricket than Ramadhin's home debut with Crompton. Crompton were playing Middleton and Ramadhin's reputation as a spinner who had mastered the best of England batsmen the previous summer needed no emphasizing. Cyril Washbrook had confessed himself unable to 'read' Ramadhin's hand. Len Hutton had found it exceedingly difficult to pick out the leg break from the googly and both Denis Compton and Bill Edrich had had their unhappy moments against him. What then would he do to Saturday afternoon batsmen? The answer was, of course, that Ramadhin was at times well nigh unplayable and he

almost carried Crompton, a weak batting side, to the championship; but against Middleton Ramadhin ran into trouble against a
teen-age left-hander who used to play for the Queen Elizabeth
Grammar School on Saturday mornings and for the Middleton
town club in the afternoons. Frank Tyson had done the same a
year or two earlier but Jimmy Hyde that early May afternoon
went out to open the Middleton innings and proceeded to hit a
delightful century without once ever appearing in difficulties
against the varied and accurate spin of Ramadhin. It was, of
course, an innings of immense promise and it earned Hyde
both a big collection and a stream of Sunday paper headlines
especially when in reply to a question: 'Did you read his hand?'
the youngster replied, truthfully and simply: 'No, I couldn't do
that – I played him on the drop. Wasn't that the natural thing to
do?'

Ramadhin still tells this story and thought highly of Hyde who
became the first amateur batsman to hit 1,000 runs in a Central
Lancashire League season for more than 35 years in that same
season; but what did Lancashire do about such a talented player?
To their credit Lancashire gave Hyde trials in the nets and at the
crease with the second team but they were not impressed and filed
his card away marked 'Uncertain in defence'! In all fairness to
those at Old Trafford who failed to see the promise of a fine and
natural hitter it must be said that the youngster himself, a talented
musician as well as a cricketer, showed no great inclination to
take up the game professionally but settled for a career in teaching
coupled with a lot of spare-time work as a successful church
organist and orchestral leader. Yet it is strange that Tyson, like
Hyde, should also fail to impress the Lancashire officials.

It was my pleasure to take this young fast bowler down to the
Old Trafford nets for a trial very early in his career and whilst he
was still at school. I left him in the junior dressing room and had
to go seek him out an hour later to lead him to the practice ground
because the officials had forgotten him. It was a bad start. What
was worse was that after Tyson had sent down only half a dozen
deliveries or so the club coach, shaking his head somewhat ruefully,
told me: 'He'll never do. He bends at the knee.' And that was

9. A typical Bradford League game. Play in progress on the picturesque ground of the Saltaire Cricket Club at Roberts Park—venue of many sterling performances by Sydney Barnes.

10. Leslie Warburton, a talented musician as well as an all-round cricketer who played for Lancashire and in a Test Trial at Lord's whilst still in league cricket.

11. Eddie Paynter, the former Lancashire and England batsman—the Lancashire League's most successful recruit to first-class cricket.

12. Learie Constantine at the height of his power with Nelson in the Lancashire League.

Frank Tyson at 16! Later I persuaded Lancashire to have another look and the man who was to become a bowler feared throughout the cricketing world was granted a second team trial at Old Trafford. Again the fates conspired against the player and the county. A back injury forced Tyson to retire after bowling only three overs . . . and that was the end of him with the county of his birth! He went, thanks to the influence of Jock Livingston, to Northamptonshire and from there to Australia and South Africa with M.C.C. teams under Len Hutton and Peter May. Imagine my feelings one gloriously sunny morning in Melbourne when Tyson, with the support of Brian Statham at the other end, routed Australia to win a Test match against the odds. Never have I seen better or more fearsome fast bowling than Tyson produced that memorable morning in Australia and my story to the *Manchester Evening News* at close of play was tinged with pride that Tyson was my discovery, and regret that Lancashire had thought fit to pass them by.

On the whole Ramadhin and the other West Indians of those vintage days were the masters of the league cricket situation. Worrell, of course, topped the 1,000 run mark with ease and the taking of 100 wickets was almost a formality for Ramadhin. It was the same in the Lancashire League where Weekes regularly compiled his centuries to top the 'thousand' mark and Walcott also demonstrated he was amongst the most prolific as well as stylish batsmen ever to grace the league cricket scene. Later there came another batch of talented West Indian cricketers led by Gary Sobers who followed Worrell to Radcliffe and confined his activities to the Central Lancashire League whereas Conrad Hunte went to Enfield and Collie Smith, whose tragic death in a road accident at the height of his career was a dreadful blow to cricket at both league and international level, joined Burnley and delighted everybody.

Wes Hall travelled to Accrington, Roy Gilchrist to Middleton and Charlie Griffith followed Smith at Burnley whilst Clive Lloyd took guard at Haslingden and Basil Butcher developed roots at Bacup where he reminded club followers so much of the heavy-scoring Weekes. Strange to relate the brilliance of Rohan Kanhai

E

was reserved first for Scotland, then for Blackpool in the Northern League and later still for Ashington in the North-east. No matter what the name or where the locality the West Indies brand of cricket was always appreciated and welcomed in the league cricketing spheres. But the Australians and the West Indians had to bear comparison to some delightful cricketers from every other cricketing land in the world. South Africa, it may well be true, were not great suppliers of league cricket professionals, but they did contribute Hugh Tayfield to East Lancashire and Eddie Barlow to Accrington. Years before they had also contributed no small part in the glories that abounded just after the first World War when they were represented by Charlie Llewellyn who also made quite a name for himself with Hampshire in between service with Lancashire League clubs.

India had allowed Amar Singh to play for Colne and Amarnath to turn out with Burnley, but the greatest Indian summers in Lancashire were undoubtedly after the second World War when Vinoo Mankad, Vijay Hazare, Dhatu Phadkar and Polly Umrigar headed a collection of great players that also included the two Guptes, both spin bowlers of tremendous appeal. Mankad first of all played for Castleton Moor where often he was on the field throughout the course of a whole match, opening the batting and staying unbeaten in an innings and then going on to bowl and field in his own inimitable manner. He was released by Haslingden, the Lancashire League club whom he joined after three years with the Moor in Central Lancashire League cricket, to play a masterly role for his country in a memorable Lord's Test match during the 1952 series when he hit 72 in the first innings, went out to bowl a marathon spell for figures of 5–196 with the ball, and then completed a great job of work with a magnificent second innings century of 184. And then he went back to Haslingden to play in a local 'derby' match against Ramsbottom and failed dismally, scoring nine runs and taking only two wickets!

The scorecard of the match (p. 68-9) tells its own story but Don Davies, a delightful writer on league cricket for the *Manchester Guardian* and a man who had played in several leagues as well as on occasions for Lancashire, was on the spot to recount the story of

Mankad's return 'home'. He wrote: 'To cock a snoot at England in a Test Match at Lord's is one thing; to tackle Ramsbottom at Ramsbottom in a Lancashire League match is "up another street tha knows". This the great Mankad found to his cost on Saturday when his share in Haslingden's victory over Ramsbottom by five wickets was – in the eyes of the massed photographers at least – a shockingly modest one. Though Mankad bowled beautifully for two hours and extracted from the local lads a degree of respect bordering on reverence, he nevertheless took only two wickets, Bowker's and Wren's, the first and the last.

'And though his batting average for ten innings at the start of the match had stood at 104, his tired blade this time could muster only nine runs – including five quiet singles and one dazzling hook shot for four – before he got himself out with a suicidal shot too ghastly to describe. Mohamed, his compatriot professional for Ramsbottom, fared little better; two wickets were his portion and a "duck" whose fashioning occupied twelve agonizing minutes. Ramsbottom batted first and before we had properly adjusted our protesting anatomies to the thin slats on which we, as spectators, were preparing to chafe and wriggle for the next five hours, a shout announced Mohamed's downfall, trapped lbw, by the first ball from the wily Gastall which had not swung away with the bowler's arm. All ruses in cricket seemingly are not of oriental origin.

'Next, with the score at 17, Chamberlain, a perfectly innocent batsman, if his face be any guide, was adjudged run out in circumstances which drew loud and conflicting opinions from two schools of thought – the one maintaining that he had been in "afe an 'eawr", the other equally emphatic that he had been run "eawt a mile". Meanwhile the batsman himself returned sadly to the pavilion bringing his griefs with him. By this time the famous but ever modest Mankad had come on to bowl and it was interesting to observe how short his run was and how economical his action and effort. His rapid sequence of overs, his quiet business-like air, and his complete absence of fuss commended itself to the practical good sense of the many women spectators.

' "Ah reckon he'll bowl three overs, Annie, while Lindwall's

ENGLAND v. INDIA
(SECOND TEST MATCH)
Played at Lord's, June 19th, 20th, 21st, 23rd and 24th, 1952
England won by 8 wickets.

First Innings	INDIA		Second Innings		
V. Mankad, c Watkins, b Trueman	..	72	b Laker	.. ..	184
P. Roy, c and b Bedser	..	35	b Bedser		0
P. R. Umrigar, b Trueman	..	5	b Trueman	.. ..	14
V. S. Hazare, not out ..	..	69	c Laker, b Bedser	..	49
V. L. Manjrekar, lbw, b Bedser ..	..	5	b Laker	.. ..	1
D. G. Phadkar, b Watkins	..	8	b Laker	.. ..	16
H. R. Adhikari, lbw, b Watkins ..	..	0	b Trueman	.. ..	16
G. S. Ramchand, b Trueman	..	18	b Trueman	.. ..	42
M. K. Mantri, b Trueman	..	1	c Compton, b Laker ..		5
S. G. Shinde, st Evans, b Watkins	..	5	c Hutton, b Trueman		14
Ghulam Ahmed, b Jenkins	..	0	not out	.. ..	1
Extras	..	17	Extras ..	..	36
Total	..	235	Total ..	..	378

Runs at the fall of each wicket—

		1	2	3	4	5	6	7	8	9	10
First Innings	..	106	116	118	126	135	139	167	180	221	235
Second Innings	..	7	59	270	272	289	312	314	323	377	378

First Innings	ENGLAND		Second Innings		
L. Hutton, c Mantri, b Hazare	..	150	not out	.. ..	39
R. T. Simpson, b Mankad	..	53	run out	.. ..	2
P. B. H. May, c Mantri, b Mankad	..	74	c Roy, b Ghulam Ahmed		26
D. C. S. Compton, lbw, b Hazare..	..	6	not out	.. ..	4
T. W. Graveney, c Mantri, b Ghulam Ahmed		73			
A. J. Watkins, b Mankad	..	0			
T. G. Evans, c and b Ghulam Ahmed	..	104			
R. O. Jenkins, st Mantri, b Mankad	..	21	Did not bat		
J. C. Laker, not out	..	23			
A. V. Bedser, c Ramchand, b Mankad	..	3			
F. S. Trueman, b Ghulam Ahmed	..	17			
Extras	..	13	Extras	.. ..	8
Total	..	537	Total (2 wkts.)	..	79

Runs at the fall of each wicket—

		1	2	3	4	5	6	7	8	9	10
First Innings	..	106	264	272	292	292	451	468	506	514	537
Second Innings	..	8	71								

The scorecards illustrating the power of Vinoo Mankad in a Test Match at Lord's—and his comparative failure in a Lancashire League match a week later.

BOWLING ANALYSIS

INDIA

First Innings	O.	M.	R.	W.	Second Innings	O.	M.	R.	W.
A. V. Bedser	33	8	62	2	A. V. Bedser	36	13	60	2
F. S. Trueman	25	3	72	4	F. S. Trueman	27	4	110	4
R. O. Jenkins	7.3	1	26	1	R. O. Jenkins	10	1	40	0
J. C. Laker	12	5	21	0	J. C. Laker	39	15	102	4
A. J. Watkins	17	7	37	3	A. J. Watkins	8	0	20	0
					D. C. S. Compton	2	0	10	0

ENGLAND

First Innings	O.	M.	R.	W.	Second Innings	O.	M.	R.	W.
D. G. Phadkar	27	8	44	0	G. S. Ramchand	1	0	5	0
G. S. Ramchand	29	8	67	0	V. S. Hazare	1	1	0	0
V. S. Hazare	24	4	53	2	V. Mankad	24	12	35	0
V. Mankad	73	24	196	5	Ghulam Ahmed	23.2	9	31	1
Ghulam Ahmed	43.4	12	106	3					
S. G. Shinde	6	0	43	0					
P. R. Umrigar	4	0	15	0					

RAMSBOTTOM v. HASLINGDEN — *Saturday June 28th., 1952.*

RAMSBOTTOM

Mohamed, Gul	lbw	Gastall	0
R. Bowker	b	Mankad	15
E. Chamberlain	run out		2
G. Barnes	b	Pilkington	15
D. Hodson	lbw	Pilkington	14
G. Marsden	b	Pilkington	9
F. Openshaw	lbw	Pilkington	10
W. Savage	b	Pilkington	4
E. Vernon	b	Pilkington	4
A. Morris	not out		13
G. Wren	c Burton	b Mankad	6
		Extras	4
			96 all out

Bowling.

T. Barnes 4.1.5.0.   Mankad V. 17-5.6.43.2.
J. W. H. Gastall 10.2.22.1.   A. Pilkington 12.3.22.6.

HASLINGDEN

Mankad, V.	b	Morris	9
J. Burton	c Vernon	b Mohamed	0
L. Pilkington	lbw	Morris	2
H. Whittaker	b	Morris	6
J. W. H. Gastall	b	Mohamed	11
A. Pilkington	not out		42
R. Scott	not out		22
		Extras	6
			98 for 5

Bowling

Mohamed 13.2.34.2.   A. Morris 9-3.0.46.3.   W. Savage 3.1.12.0.

walking back to his place. Ah canno' do wi' o' that palaver, com yo'?" Annie couldn't. Nor could she deny some sympathy with the batsmen in their cramped efforts to deal with Mankad's subtly varied slows to a tightly set field. "He's overawn 'em, Maggie. Look at o' them chaps round t'batter. Ah'd be that feart, wouldn't yo'?" Maggie would for sure; and so, apparently, were most of the Ramsbottom batsmen, since the whole eleven of them could only muster 96 hesitant runs. Mankad's achievement on Saturday, if any, lay in the moral field. Though he took only two wickets himself he exerted a kind of hypnotic influence which paralysed enterprise and left the batsmen psychologically ready to fall into Pilkington's traps at the other end. Pilkington bowled cunningly for his six wickets. He sensed from Mankad the wearing-down value of a pitiless length and seemed to know instinctively just when a batsman had decided to throw discretion to the winds, pin his ears back, and try to satisfy the gentleman at long-off who had been a stentorian advocate of free-scoring methods all afternoon.

'Pilkington foxed two of his victims with yorkers, two were lbw – all through swinging too soon at his slower, hanging, ball – while length and top spin did for the rest. He no doubt went into the pavilion at the close of Ramsbottom's innings feeling satisfied that Old Kaspar's work was done "at onny road fer one day" and that the putting on of pads was a remote possibility for him. But by the time J. Burton had been brilliantly caught behind the wicket off Mohamed, and L. Pilkington, Mankad and H. Whittaker were all wondering how they had fallen to the boyish Morris for 21 beggarly runs we saw A. Pilkington, the bowler, once more emerging into the sunlight to play the part of a Maurice Leyland and squash the incipient panic. That Pilkington had been preordained for such a glorious part seemed clear from the moment when Marsden dropped an easy catch from him at long leg, the score then being 38. As always happens Pilkington now found runs easy to make and R. Scott, his last partner, found his air of confidence so infectious as to feel encouraged to add twenty carefree runs, not out, himself. Together this pair knocked off the 55 runs needed to win the match, with a margin that at one hideous moment seemed most unlikely.'

That was one of the greatest examples of the ups and the downs of a cricketer's life. Year after year Mankad roamed the world playing and coaching cricket. He spent some fifteen years in England in the Lancashire, Central Lancashire and Bolton Leagues, leaving behind him a legend of great batting and superb bowling performances. It was said of him that he was a team in himself and certainly it was his good luck to possess all-round skill equal to any player, anywhere and in any era.

Mankad stood out head and shoulders above the rest of the Indian contingent who graced league cricket simply because the others could not match Mankad's ability to get both runs and wickets. Always they proved match-winning and crowd-pleasing cricketers but Mankad was in a class, almost a world, of his own.

Pakistan made their contribution when Fazal Mahmood came to East Lancashire and later Hanif Mohammed to Crompton and there were others like Saeed Ahmed (Nelson), Alimuddin (Heywood), and Ikram Elahi (Haslingden).

The New Zealand contribution, small though it was, included before the war C. S. 'Stewie' Dempster, Bill Merritt and Ted Badcock. Afterwards John Reid spent three memorable years at Heywood where his ability to bowl seamers accurately and bat with delightful ease and power brought him runs and wickets in sufficient quantity to enable him to join the select band of 'double' performers who took 100 wickets or more and hit more than 1,000 runs in a season.

Reid, in point of fact, was sorely tempted at one time to stay in England. League clubs were always pressing for his services and one or two counties joined in the bid, for he was probably the best all-rounder New Zealand has ever produced. In the end he decided to return home and skipper his country in many Test matches against England, South Africa and Australia – a great player and a sterling example to the youth not only of his own country but wherever he played at league or first-class level. A serious knee injury shortened his career but wherever the talk is of cricket in Lancashire the name of John Reid is coupled with the greatest players from all parts of the world.

Chapter 9

The Opposition at Home

It does not follow that because of the strength of the overseas invasion in league cricket there was no opportunity for English born players, yet as the years wore on, there was less and less inclination on the part of the Lancashire League clubs to employ 'home' labour. It had become the fashion to go farther afield but there were, of course, some good players from our counties. Before World War II there were many league professionals in this country who could hold their own or, at least, provide a challenge to the Australians, the West Indians and the others from overseas. Leslie Warburton was the prime example. There were others and in the smaller leagues where the money available would seldom stretch far enough to passage money as well as salary for the 'foreigners' there was a brisk 'trade' in English born cricketers.

The Yorkshiremen who caught the Saturday morning special from Leeds and Bradford were all welcome on the Lancashire cricketing scene and many of them regularly produced performances denoting skill above the ordinary. But what, one might well ask, was Lancashire's contribution to her own domestic cricketing scene? There were plenty of good cricketers who migrated from the ground staff at Old Trafford to the leagues and the county club was ever ready to provide a substitute professional at long or short notice. When injuries and illness overtook the big-name players the clubs had little or no alternative but to go to the Lancashire headquarters for help – and it was usually forthcoming at a very reasonable fee. In point of fact there was quite a steady flow of ground-staff players to the leagues on their own volition.

Such was the strength of county cricket at Old Trafford between the two wars that vacancies in the senior side were few and far between, and young players who joined the staff with high ambition soon got tired of waiting for their chance and settled for a steady job in league cricket. Jack Holroyd was a case in point. This shrewd left-hander who bowled his spinners with all the guile of a master could never force his way into the Lancashire side although there was a marked absence of his variety of spin at the time. When Holroyd did get a chance with Lancashire he was usually unlucky with the state of the pitch and the strength of the opposition. And so he came into the leagues. He spent several seasons with Haslingden in the Lancashire League and was never far from the top of the bowling averages. He then moved over to Ashton in the Central Lancashire League where again he produced figures that brought success far oftener than failure. Maybe Holroyd's batting was not really good enough for the highly competitive cricketing world but 'Tich' was always a professional to be respected and, when conditions favoured him as frequently they did in Saturday afternoon matches, he could be as deadly as any of his overseas rivals.

Year in and year out, throughout the 1930s and the 1940s Jack Holroyd spun out batsmen, and when wickets eluded him, kept the best batsmen in the leagues quiet. His easy action and ability to drop the ball on the spot that mattered were allied to a good humour and placid temperament that made him a cricketer much sought after by the clubs where money was limited but hope sprang eternal. Reg Parkin, son of the more famous Cecil, was another league cricketer of repute between the two wars. His off-spinners often 'bit' deep into the turf and into the ranks of the opposing batsmen and he was also able to bat well enough to reach regularly the 500 runs-a-season mark.

Steve Preston, a giant of a man who bowled fast and hit remarkably hard, was another who, tired of waiting for his chance at Old Trafford, turned to the leagues and enjoyed a happy spell at Middleton who later discovered a left-hander they considered capable of following in the footsteps of the immortal Hedley Verity. Eric Denison was his name and had not war broken out at the end of the 1939 season the Moonrakers might well have provided another talented all-rounder for Yorkshire. Denison was a much better batsman than Verity and he came from the same small village, Rawdon, ten miles from Leeds, one of those hamlets where cricket was not so much a sport but a way of life. It says much for the knowledgeable Middleton officials that they spotted the promise of Denison after he had spent just one season in another League.

Years before they had gone to Accrington to take note of Verity's potential. This time a couple of the club's officials, old players, travelled to Kendal on the edge of the Lake District to run the rule over a player who had been recommended by Verity as of 'great promise'. Satisfied with what they saw Middleton lost no time in signing up a 21-year-old all-rounder who settled down so well in Central Lancashire League cricket that he became, in 1939, the first club professional to score a thousand runs in a season. And he also got more than 80 wickets with his mixture of left-hand spin and swing. Denison did so well at Towncroft that Yorkshire once again took notice. They blooded him in second team matches and made a note of his promise. With Verity at the top of his form and Frank Smales and Ellis Robinson on hand for the other kind of spin, there was little hope of Denison breaking through like Verity himself, but Yorkshire were satisfied they had a cricketer for future reference.

Alas, along came the war. Eric Denison was, in point of fact, a prisoner of war who escaped in Italy and had to live on the run for the better part of three years before he was able to return to England and to cricket. His thoughts, naturally, were on rejoining Middleton in readiness for the 1946 season but unfortunately the club officials, unaware of Denison's whereabouts or fitness, had made other professional arrangements when a much greyer and much thinner Yorkshireman once again got in touch with the club. It was a dreadful situation for both the club and the player. Torn between a desire to honour a contract with another player and an obligation to an old servant the club was in a quandary. They gave Denison a couple of games towards the close of the 1945 season and fitted him out once again with all the equipment a talented player needed. Then they decided, with great reluctance, to let him move on and promised all aid possible in securing him another professional post.

It was not difficult and Werneth jumped at the chance. Denison soon showed that a five-year break had not seriously impaired his ability but, strange to relate, Yorkshire then considered him too old although they were relying upon Arthur Booth, who was much older, for their left-hand spin when first-class cricket re-opened. Although Denison's chance of following in the footsteps of Verity, the man he regarded as an ideal cricketer, had gone he stayed on to make telling contributions for several clubs in several leagues. He had a spell in the Lancashire League with Todmorden and broke a club batting record before returning to the Central Lancashire League with Royton and then moving on to do service in the Bolton and Huddersfield Leagues.

Combining playing with coaching Denison was probably the first cricketer in Lancashire to persuade local education authorities that cricket had a place in their scheme for 'further education' in the winter months and he took charge of an indoor school at Oldham where many good youngsters were taught the basic principles of good cricket long before the MCC formed their Youth Council and set up blue-prints for similar schools up and down the country. Some of Denison's earliest pupils went on to become county and test cricketers. Keith Andrew, the Northamptonshire and England wicket-keeper, was one. Malcolm Hilton and Geoff Pullar, of Lancashire and England, were others. The Lancashire County Cricket Club expressed their gratitude to Denison by inviting him to become one of their first official talent spotters. Unfortunately his recommendations often fell on unsympathetic ears and several good young players were lost to the county through a lack of administrative organization and failure to encourage and assist in the making of cricketers.

Lancashire's need at the time was for immediate replacements of experienced players and they appeared to lack both the patience to wait for Denison's recruits to mature and the necessity for offering the same youngsters some form of security. Nonetheless, like one or two other Yorkshiremen, Denison did his best to spotlight the faults of the Red Rose system and went a long way to helping eradicate them. It was not his fault that, when he moulded the raw material into shape, the county authorities failed to take over and complete the job – and it was a failure that cost Lancashire dearly in terms of promising young cricketers lost to the game or denied the opportunity to pursue it beyond the league level.

Denison's career record of more than 15,000 runs and 1,500 wickets in league cricket is a proud one and there have been few better Saturday afternoon cricketers. It was his misfortune that war stopped play when his future was rich in promise but there were many others in the same position and I do not think Denison considered himself any more unlucky than the rest. Rather did he strive to make up for lost time and I am sure had Yorkshire given him another chance when Booth retired after only a season and a half in first-class cricket this Rawdon left-hander would have made the grade and delighted the cricketing public over a far wider area. Yorkshire's loss was league cricket's gain.

Chapter 10

The Cost of Professionalism

It is an unwritten law in the leagues of Lancashire that the amount of money paid to the professionals is not for publication. Many an old-timer has replied to my questioning on this point to the effect; 'Mind thi own business. What we pay our pro is up to us and to him. Would tha like to see thi's own wages made public?' It is an argument I would not quibble with but it has led to much speculation about what the top-class professional can earn in a season of Lancashire League cricket. I stress Lancashire League cricket because that is the one sphere where big money is undoubtedly available. And in spite of a falling-off in crowd figures and the ever-encroaching menace of football it is still possible for the Lancashire League professional to earn more money for week-end appearances than can be obtained for first-class cricket seven days a week.

I believe it is fair to assert that Ray Lindwall is so far the highest paid league professional. Nelson, who brought the world famous fast bowler from Australia to this country in 1950, do not deny it cost them a fee of four figure proportions and another £400 to get the player and his wife to England from their Brisbane home. Yet is was considered a very sound investment for Lindwall was as good and as an attractive a professional as any who ever graced the League. He was not the only cricketer to earn over £1,000 for a season of league cricket. It is freely admitted in Lancashire League circles that in addition to Lindwall fellow Australians like Colin McCool and Bruce Dooland who played for East Lancashire were in the higher income bracket. So, too, was Hugh Tayfield, the South African off-spinner, who had a disappointing season with the same club.

Wes Hall and Charlie Griffith, the formidable West Indies fast

EXPENDITURE ACCOUNT FOR 1

EXPENDITURE	1955 £	s.	d.	1954 £	s.	d.
To Stock of Club Ties, 3/10/1954 ..	27	6	6	—	—	—
„ Hire of Rooms	0	15	0	0	17	6
„ Cricket Coaching—Evening School	7	0	0	6	0	0
„ Donations	17	7	0	5	19	0
„ Wages	816	11	0	723	2	9
„ Ground Repairs and Renewals ..	57	12	3	91	18	11
„ Insurances	30	9	0	29	3	9
„ Ground Expenses	149	13	9	63	14	9
„ Cricket Equipment and Repairs ..	97	2	2	89	13	4
„ Rates and Taxes	65	19	2	43	4	0
„ Match Expenses	171	13	10	193	1	6
„ Umpires	49	10	11	45	5	6
„ Printing, Stationery and Advertising	112	8	5	110	0	5
„ Talent Money and Seasons Prizes	29	10	4	20	19	0
„ Gas, Water and Electricity	31	16	10	27	16	0
„ Postages and Telephones	25	10	3	26	9	1
„ Scorers and Number Boys ..	18	17	3	16	12	3
„ Gatemen and Checkers	20	12	9	20	16	3
„ Programmes—Cost	114	0	0	120	0	0
„ C.L.L. Subscription..	5	5	0	10	5	0
„ C.L.L. Dinners	8	2	6	3	6	0
„ C.L.L. Handbooks	2	13	0	1	13	0
„ Grant—Ladies' Committee ..	10	0	0	10	0	0
„ Secretaries' Honorariums	45	0	0	45	0	0
„ Sundry Expenses	12	11	0	7	11	4
„ Bank Charges	5	9	10	6	15	6
„ Second Eleven Grant	5	0	0	5	0	0
„ Purchase of Club Ties	—	—	—	31	1	0
„ Police Supervision at Matches ..	—	—	—	3	17	0
„ Presentation Case—F. Tyson ..	—	—	—	11	1	0
„ Balance—Surplus for year, 1955 ..	644	19	1	67	1	11
	£2582	16	10	£1837	5	9

A typical League cricket club balance sheet – note the wages item tha

R ENDING 31ST OCTOBER, 1955

		1955			1954		
INCOME		£	s.	d.	£	s.	d.
By Subscriptions		551	19	6	520	15	6
„ Tennis Club Rental		15	0	0	15	0	0
„ Hockey Club Rental ..		20	0	0	20	0	0
„ Gate Receipts—League		721	16	0	453	9	9
„ „ Wood Cup (Net) ..		445	13	2	102	4	10
„ „ Whittaker Cup (Net)		0	15	1	—	—	—
„ Garden Rents		2	9	6	3	0	0
„ Ladies' Committee—Pavilion Side		149	13	0	185	14	2
„ „ E. Kay, Tea Hut		155	0	0	95	3	0
„ Donations		15	5	0	10	0	0
„ Social Efforts		266	12	3	207	15	10
„ Programmes—Sales and Adverts ..		211	6	10	192	10	8
„ Sale of Club Ties		7	7	0	4	5	6
„ Stock of Club Ties, 31/10/1955 ..		19	19	6	27	6	6

Audited and found correct from the Books, Vouchers, and information furnished to us. We have to report that on October 31st, 1955, subscriptions amounting to £10 19s. 6d. were still unpaid. The value of Timber for New Seating in stock on 31st October was £127 6s. 6d.

Signed: K. ARMITAGE,

E. SCOTT,

Honorary Auditors to the Middleton Cricket Club.

7th November, 1955.

£2582 16 10   £1837 5 9

ofessional's salary with that of the groundsman and other paid help.

bowling pair, were also highly paid professionals when they played for Accrington and Burnley respectively and in more recent years I believe Bob Cowper, the all-rounder from New South Wales, cost East Lancashire a four-figure fee as well as the fare to and from Sydney. Because they never signed for Lancashire League clubs it is probable that neither Frank Worrell nor Gary Sobers earned that much with Radcliffe but they undoubtedly did so when they left the Central Lancashire League to play in the Staffordshire area; and I believe, as do many other Central Lancashire league followers, that when Charles Barnett was at Rochdale he was the best paid player in that league's history although Cec Pepper and Dhatu Phadkar, both former Rochdale professionals, must have run him close.

Where does the money come from? Gate receipts do not always cover the professionals' salary but most league clubs base their bargaining power on the strength of guaranteed income from membership – the bigger the membership the more money that can be made available for a professional. Often a club has a wealthy sponsor who is willing to contribute to the costs of the professional or stand guarantee at the bank should the season prove a wet one and the professional unattractive, but it says much for the business instincts of club officials that seldom do they have to go cap in hand to either bank or sponsor to make ends meet.

Membership is basically of several grades. Vice-presidents are the 'elite' among the club supporters. They pay extra to denote their willingness to contribute and their annual donations may be anything from three guineas to ten guineas. Ordinary membership varies from three or four guineas to as little as one guinea at the smaller clubs and there are also reduced fees for ladies and juniors as well as for old-age pensioners who now prefer to be known as 'senior citizens'. Often there is also recourse to special efforts to balance the books for although the annual balance sheets of the clubs are models of straight-forward accountancy, they seldom disclose the amount paid to the professional. The annual 'wages' item usually covers the groundsman as well as the professional and it may also include the cost of a steward or bartender. The Lancashire League maintains a strong control over its paid players

13. The East Lancashire Cricket Club ground at Alexandra Meadows, Blackburn.

14. Charles Barnett, the former Gloucestershire and England all-rounder did a great job for Rochdale in the Central Lancashire League.

15. Eric Denison, a Central Lancashire League professional who might have played for Yorkshire and England but for the Second World War.

16. The late Sir Frank Worrell, a batsman who delighted the crowds in the Central Lancashire and Staffordshire leagues.

and insists upon two essential clauses being inserted in all contracts which must be deposited with the League Secretary as a mark of good faith season after season.

In their wisdom the League has seen fit to demand that 'the said . . . . . shall not at any time during the continuance of this agreement play in any cricket match other than the matches organized by his own club, or in a friendly game in which the players of the said club are engaged, or in matches where the said . . . . . is engaged to play as substitute professional or in matches arranged by or agreed to by the Committee of the Lancashire League'.

The League also insists 'a professional shall be engaged for the whole season and must be available for all League and Worsley Cup matches, and a club shall not substitute any other professional except in case of absolute inability of the professional to play owing to illness or similar cause'. These two clauses safeguard the interest of the clubs who are otherwise free to make what stipulations they wish in their contracts with professionals and it is seldom that either a club or the League Committee has to step in to enforce the rules and conditions laid down. Professionalism is certainly not undertaken lightly in any league and the system works well with clubs and players abiding by the letter and the spirit of the agreements which are often drawn up by legal advisers who are club members and usually acting in an honorary capacity. I certainly cannot remember a club or a player clashing on the fundamental issues necessitating court action and although there have been occasions when the professionals have been 'disciplined' for breach of rule or contract this seldom calls for the intervention of the League or the law.

In the old days professionals were also groundsmen but this doubling of jobs is no longer possible except in the smaller leagues and a club is well satisfied if its professional can gather in the runs, take the wickets, and pull in the crowds. It is in the interest of both the club and the professional to do so for collections for meritorious performances are extras to a player's salary and on good days could bring in another £30 or so as a reward for attractive batting or destructive bowling. In some cases the pro-

F

fessional may find local employment that does not interfere with his cricketing duties and thus further boost his income. Many professional cricketers can also arrange to do some day-time coaching at schools or colleges in which case he can, all in all, make good money. None did better than Tony Lock, the former England, Surrey, Leicestershire and Western Australian left-arm bowler, who played one season for Ramsbottom and also made mid-week appearances with Leicestershire before going there as captain. Ramsbottom is in reality little more than a village club, yet it was possible to pay Lock a four-figure fee to produce a dynamic brand of week-end cricket that not only brought in big crowds but also doubled the club membership.

There are really no limits to the lengths an enterprising league club will go to obtain the services of the very best players as professionals and it is seldom they fail in their objective although two of England's best fast bowlers recently resisted big offers to play Lancashire League cricket. East Lancashire made a determined effort to lure Brian Statham into their ranks with a four-figure offer, but he refused it partly on grounds of business interests elsewhere and upon the fact that 'I would get very little pleasure out of bowling fast against young teenage cricketers just starting out on their careers'. This, surely, was a unique and commendable thought by a cricketer who could not have failed to dominate league cricket. Likewise several Lancashire League clubs made overtures to Freddie Trueman when he announced his retirement from the first-class game. In the Yorkshireman's case even the wealthiest of league clubs could not compete with the offers he received and accepted to turn journalist and stage comedian. Statham and Trueman apart, the Lancashire League clubs, like the Canadian Mounties usually get their man!

Chapter 11

A Telling Contribution

There was a strange reluctance on the part of the Lancashire league clubs to engage county cricketers as club professionals when their time came for retiring from first-class cricket, and it is even stranger that such Lancashire stalwarts as Dick Pollard and John Ikin were allowed to end their careers in the Birmingham and Staffordshire Leagues respectively. Occasionally there was a breakthrough. Milnrow brought 'Dusty' Rhodes into the Central Lancashire League for a brief spell and Littleborough engaged Eddie Phillipson for a season or two but even at a later stage there were no offers for such a talented player as Roy Tattersall when the England off-spinner was somewhat prematurely asked to leave Old Trafford. Like Pollard he went to the Birmingham League but Malcolm Hilton was luckier. He found employment with Burnley and Oldham.

The league clubs could, in general, and should be more sympathetic to their own county players when they are no longer wanted by Lancashire. The majority of them would, I feel sure, do well enough on the field and at the nets to justify engagement and the good work of Ken Grieves at Stockport, Accrington and Milnrow since leaving Old Trafford is a pointer to what might be achieved. Even if Lancashire had little to offer, the rest of the English counties generally had cricketers capable of doing a grand job in the leagues and to my mind none did more to prove the point than the old Gloucestershire and England player, Charles Barnett, who joined Rochdale after turning down a Middleton offer of £850 to accept terms generally believed to be more than £1,000. Barnett was one of the highest paid Central Lancashire League cricketers of all time and he came into the league when there was world-class opposition all around him.

Frank Worrell was at Radcliffe, George Tribe at Milnrow, Jock Livingston at Royton, John Reid at Heywood and Sonny Ramadhin at Crompton. Barnett was at ease in this class. He got runs in his own attractive style and took wickets regularly with his medium-paced seamers that often went unrecognized by Gloucestershire and England. In addition Barnett proved himself a superb fieldsman and a master tactician in Central Lancashire League cricket. He built up a Rochdale side that was as good as any in any era and he did it by example and by undertaking the job in all its aspects. Charles Barnett was a throw-back to the old days. He was a cricketer of great talent and he believed that by coming into the league he had more to do than score runs and take wickets. He was interested in winning matches and titles, of course, but above all else he was determined Rochdale's money should be well spent and he insisted upon spending at least three nights a week at the nets. What is more important Barnett made it quite clear to his employers that unless he got full co-operation in his determined bid to create a cricketing atmosphere of dedication and loyalty he was wasting his time. No matter how good a player was he was expected to attend the nets twice a week or risk being left out of the side.

Although he continued to live in his native Gloucestershire Barnett never failed to spend the major portion of his working week in Rochdale. He found and encouraged a group of young players who thrived under his leadership. Although he was not named as captain of the side there was never any doubt who was leading it – and it was a good thing for Rochdale in particular and the Central Lancashire League in general that such a state of affairs should be permitted and encouraged. What is the use, after all, of engaging a top-class player as club professional if he cannot carry out his job to the limit of his capabilities? Barnett was, undoubtedly, one of the few English cricketers of his day who could play alongside such stylish opponents as Worrell, Weekes and Walcott and not suffer by comparison. But that was not enough. Barnett's object in turning to league cricket was to pass on the benefit of experience gained at the highest cricketing level and he meant his influence to stay with his club for years after he had gone.

He never failed to stress the value of good fielding or the need for physical fitness. He was not interested in scoring runs for the sake of the record books. Neither did he regard it as essential his name should appear at the top of the batting and bowling averages either for his club or his league. What Charles Barnett wanted more than anything else was to encourage and inspire the younger generation of players. How well he succeeded can be gauged from the fact that for years after he had gone the Rochdale side were always to the fore in Central Lancashire League cricket.

It was said of Barnett when he was at Rochdale that he was an idealist. Maybe he was. Certainly he once upset quite a few league officials by speaking his mind at the Rochdale club's annual dinner. Barnett had come to collect a medal or a cup won on the field of play the previous season but he took the opportunity to chide league cricket generally and the Lancashire and Central Lancashire Leagues in particular for ignoring the English-born professional. It was his belief that every county club could supply on demand an old cricketer capable of doing an ideal league cricket job. But he did not mean, and he stressed this, that they should hit up runs by the thousand or take wickets by the hundred. That was not the Barnett way although, of course, he seldom failed to do both at Rochdale.

What he thought and what he boldly inferred was that the leagues were living in a fool's paradise. He did not say so in as many words but there was no mistaking his views when asked what a club could gain from paying big money for overseas professionals who would produce staggering figures with bat or ball – occasionally with both – but then go on their way using those figures as a means of getting still more money from clubs that inevitably bid for their services? 'Would it not be better, both from the club's point of view and for cricket,' asked Barnett, 'that the professional should do more lasting good and leave behind him several young players of promise to remain and delight the club members and followers?' It was a pertinent point and it was sound cricket advice from a master player who had several times stood aside at Rochdale and allowed the amateurs to take over the winning of a match.

Barnett believed that the leagues of Lancashire were sacrificing

the substance of good cricket for the shadow of shattering performances and big newspaper headlines for world-famous players
carrying all before them. These men, he argued, were playing out
of their class and doing no lasting good for the game. He did not
blame the professionals for he said bluntly they had been engaged
for that purpose and were fulfilling their obligations to the letter.
He put the blame on the men who were listening to him, the club
officials who could see no farther than next year's championship or
Cup success. He warned them the public would get tired of this
kind of cricket and pleaded for a more commonsense approach
with the simple request the game be allowed to remain of far
greater importance than the player.

Barnett was a brave man to say what he did for he was probably
earning as much if not more than many of his overseas professional
colleagues and left himself open to criticism. Yet none, with the
real interest of cricket at heart, could fail to see his point of view
and in recent years the truth of his words must have come forcibly
home to roost in many a league cricket committee room.

The fault did not lie with the professionals. They performed
their duties to the best of their ability and to the letter of their
contract. What was wrong, as Barnett inferred, was that committees
had got their priorities wrong. A cricketer of Frank Worrell's
stature and majesty had far more to offer than a century every
other week and a few wickets in between. Yet his club, Radcliffe,
was not only well pleased but highly delighted when the great
West Indies all-rounder accomplished the double of 1,000 runs and
100 wickets with several weeks of the season remaining. It was the
same in later years when Gary Sobers took over from Worrell to
shatter all previous returns and completely dominate the Central
Lancashire scene. And yet Radcliffe's record in terms of championships and cup successes have been few and far between.

What does it profit a club to have a professional outpacing all
others with bat and ball if his amateur colleagues have neither the
opportunity nor the ability to give him the right support? This, in
a nutshell, was what Charles Barnett was preaching years ago but
his words fell on deaf ears. Because of this the Central Lancashire
League clubs nowadays cannot afford to compete with the Lanca-

shire League in the bid for the world's cricketing stars. The crowds have gone. And it is harder than ever to persuade the youngsters of today that league cricket is a game worth playing. One of the reasons is that, when schoolboys, they watched, with awe and undoubted admiration, as the overseas players hammered up their centuries or grabbed their wickets but, at the same time, realized the amateurs in the side were being denied a real opportunity to play their part in the game. It was not Barnett who said it but I am sure he would have added a fervent 'hear, hear' to a remark that the league game was becoming less and less a sporting spectacle and more and more a variety act with the rival professionals the top-of-the-bill performers and the rest of the cast just filling in.

Chapter 12

The Trend Continues

In spite of Barnett's words and his magnificent example of what could be achieved by the right blend of performance and coaching the leagues maintained their feverish search for the big names. When the Gloucestershire man moved from Rochdale he went into the Staffordshire League and so, too, did Worrell and later Sobers and it was from here that the main competition to the Lancashire League dominance came. The Staffordshire League, for example, won the battle to sign Jim Laker when the Surrey and England off-spinner left the first-class game. He preferred to sign for Norton although it was said he was offered better terms by a Lancashire club. Perhaps the demands of the Staffordshire League clubs were not so great as were those of the Lancashire League. Certainly there were fewer match commitments in the Potteries and little or no demand for coaching duties. This undoubtedly fitted in better with Laker's business plans for he was able to continue living and working in London, travelling to the midlands to fulfil his cricketing obligations either on the Friday night or Saturday morning and returning on the Saturday evening. In the Lancashire leagues there were often mid-week Cup matches, Sunday engagements and coaching sessions to fit in and far from being a spare-time occupation league cricket was a demanding and nearly full-time job.

This suited the overseas players. They came a long way to do a job and gave it top priority and one of the reasons why the English professional often found it difficult to secure an engagement was his preoccupation with another job during the week. There were men, of course, who could accept offers and did. Johnny Wardle, the Yorkshire and England left-hander, soon found himself sought after by the league clubs when he ended his first-class career in a sensational manner and Tony Lock found it profitable enough to return from Australia to take over as Ramsbottom's professional and then move back into county cricket with Leicestershire.

Wardle had successful spells with Nelson and Rishton and proved an attractive professional with his variety of spin and his ability to hit hard with the bat. Lock, too, enjoyed much success at Ramsbottom, and it is perhaps not mere coincidence that both these England cricketers were also magnificent fieldsmen and superb showmen. Wardle was often criticized for his 'comical interludes' in first-class cricket but in the Lancashire League his antics were always regarded as part and parcel of his crowd-pulling power. At Ramsbottom, and wherever the side went, Lock was always sure to thrill the crowd with his own fiery brand of fielding and catching coupled, should the occasion arise, with a series of blood-curdling appeals for lbw or catches at the wicket. Yes, showmanship helps in league cricket.

It would be unjust, however, to suggest that this was why Lock and Wardle held their own with the overseas opposition. Their cricketing ability was the prime factor and the enthusiasm with which they went about their job. Temperamentally each was ideally suited to the league demands. They were allowed full play of their talents. Long spells of bowling, an opportunity to bat far higher than was their custom in the first-class sphere, and a major say in field placings and tactics generally brought both Lock and Wardle to the forefront match after match and week by week. Each knew failure but success was generally within their reach and it is of no little significance that each knew and went out of his way to impress upon their amateur colleagues the value of good fielding. I saw Lock play an early game for Ramsbottom as a substitute professional, and after he had three or four catches dropped the England player began to demonstrate in no uncertain manner what he felt about this lack of support.

When he took over as the club's fully-fledged professional he certainly made it his business to see the standard was improved and Ramsbottom soon became the best fielding side in the league. That was a distinct feather in Lock's cricketing cap. Ray Lindwall ran up against the same indifference to fielding when he was finally tempted to go to Nelson. In his very first match he saw two or three catches dropped behind the wicket and in the slips in his opening overs and after a spell showed traces of dissatisfaction by snatching his sweater somewhat impatiently from the umpire. His mannerisms did not pass unnoticed and an old-timer sitting on the front row of the Seedhouse pavilion, a spot he had occupied for nearly a generation, loudly warned the famous Australian fast bowler: 'It sarves thi reet, tha should bowl at bloody wickets!'

The lesson, however, did not go unheeded and long before the season was half-way through Lindwall had sacrificed pace for accuracy and was less reliant upon his fieldsmen. Roy Gilchrist, the West Indies fast bowler, had a similar experience when Middleton broke with tradition by engaging a big-name professional to win the championship and draw in the crowds, for the temperamental Gilchrist could always be relied upon to produce fireworks of one kind or another. More sinned against than sinning on many occasions Gilchrist and Middleton had a stormy relationship and twice opposing teams marched off the field in protest against the dynamic West Indian's bumpers, bouncers and beamers. In each case the blame was laid at the feet of the bowler but later there was evidence to support an opinion that opposing captains had been 'got at' to produce sensational Sunday paper headlines.

Throughout his first season at Towncroft Gilchrist was the target for the barrackers but when his final figures were analysed he had taken 140 wickets at less than ten runs each and hit the stumps 110 times. That was performance of great cricketing merit yet I seldom saw it advanced in Gilchrist's favour. He was always accused of being a dangerous bowler, one who was always dropping the ball short or zooming it through the air head high. If he could hit the stumps 110 times in 26 matches there was not much wrong with his length or direction. Yet Middleton's venture was a disaster financially. The side won the league championship in each of Gilchrist's two seasons but they reported losses of over £800 each time and went back to their old habit of going for the unknown. They signed Basil D'Oliveira to succeed Gilchrist!

The coming of the coloured South African was not without

irony. He joined Middleton on my recommendation – and I made it with trepidation. For two years I had, at the request of John Arlott, been trying to interest various league clubs in a South African coloured all-rounder who had astounding figures to his name back home in the non-European cricket of Capetown. Fantastic stories of centuries hit in less than an hour with two-thirds of the runs coming from mighty sixes – of devastating bowling returns producing figures of 7–10 or even better – of shattering feats in the field – and, above all, of the tremendous appeal this cricketer had in his own little sporting world. The trouble was there were very few means of comparing D'Oliveira and his performances with the standards he would have to face in league cricket.

His financial demands were modest enough. What he really craved was an opportunity to break out from the shackles that tied him in his native land. I was anxious to help and pleaded hard with several clubs to take a chance on D'Oliveira. Finally Middleton agreed. They were in financial stress but had seen the overseas cricketer was a crowd-puller. Gilchrist had been expensive and explosive. What they really wanted was a man from abroad anxious to make an impression yet agreeable to accept a modest salary in order that they could keep faith with their supporters and recoup some of their losses. D'Oliveira filled the bill admirably. They empowered me to offer him £450 all-in for a one-season engagement. It meant the South African would have to pay his own fare and make a quick impression if he wanted to make a go of things. It was a tall order. A very tall order indeed but when I met D'Oliveira in London and took him north he at once appealed as a sincere and deep-thinking man who knew what he wanted and was prepared to fight for it.

He arrived at the height of an apartheid squabble yet maintained silence on a subject that must have been very close to him. He looked bewildered and probably was when met by a group of news-gathering reporters more interested in South Africa's racial problems than his own cricketing ones. Fortunately I rescued him in time to make him feel he was not without friends and on the journey back to Manchester I tried hard to find out what really made this well-mannered South African tick. He said little except in answer to my many questions but he had baffled me by asking 'Where do I sit' and then 'Where do I eat,' when we boarded the train north. It was only then I fully realized the way in which the coloured South African is treated back home. Finding himself treated as an equal by white people must have come as a bigger shock to D'Oliveira than I imagined and for weeks he went around as though in a dream.

I liked him but, like everybody at Middleton, waited anxiously for him to show what he could do. His first appearance at the nets brought photographers from newspapers and television and I have often wondered since whether these fellows really knew what they were doing. I am positive their brief was not to get cricketing snaps but just pictures of a coloured South African suddenly turned loose in the bigger world of unfettered cricket. Frankly I was disappointed with D'Oliveira when he batted for half an hour and bowled for a similar spell; he appeared to be a cricketer out of his depth. That, of course, was exactly what he was. He had played all his cricket and earned his tremendous reputation back home either on matting pitches or rough-and-ready turf ones that had plenty of pace. The difference between conditions at home and those at Middleton in early April were just about as wide a cricketing gulf as one could imagine and D'Oliveira has been honest enough to confess in his autobiography that he, too, felt he had stepped into another world. He soon realized that here he was, far from home and mixing with people about whose way of life he knew nothing, being looked upon as a professional – not only from the cricketing point of view but also from every other viewpoint. Yet he survived.

In his first match D'Oliveira got few runs and few wickets. It was obvious he had a lot to learn but he had already proved one point: he was a thinker and a fighter who meant to succeed. But he was anxious, perhaps too anxious, to please and he was more than a little bewildered by the conditions. However he had one saving grace. He never made the same mistake twice. He learned from his own errors and reasoned things out for himself. He never really sought advice but eagerly accepted it when it was proffered and accounted himself a lucky man to be a member of a team of good fellows as well as good cricketers. He slowly but surely got on terms with himself and settled in to impress everybody by his obvious sincerity and appreciation of the chance he had been given.

His first half-century must have been a source of considerable delight to him. Certainly it was greeted with tremendous enthusiasm both in the dressing room and in the committee room at Middleton where, in the first few weeks, there had been considerable misgivings about the success of the new professional. In his own book D'Oliveira tells of feeling homesick and despondent until he realized everybody was willing him to success. He regarded himself as inferior to the amateurs he played alongside and in his first letter home described himself as 'a proper Charlie' both from the cricket and the domestic point of view. Fortunately by the time the 1960 season had reached the half-way stage the Middleton players and officials were beginning to accord D'Oliveira the respect due to the club's professional.

This was important to him! By the end of the season D'Oliveira had hit 930 runs for an average of 48 and taken 71 wickets at a cost of only eleven runs each. His improvement began the day the chairman of the club assured him he was proving satisfactory in every way and proved it by offering him re-engagement terms. This offer, coming only seven or eight weeks after leaving home, made Basil D'Oliveira a happy man and a contented one. He could then afford to put his doubts aside and concentrate on improving his cricket. By studious attention to detail and a quick realization of what was prudent and what was rash, and with the help of his amateur colleagues at the nets and in the middle, a cricketing miracle began to take shape.

It had taken a whip round among the coloured players at home to get D'Oliveira to England and he went back determined to repay his friends for their support by coaching and playing once again for his local club and putting into practice what he had learned the hard way in the Central Lancashire League. He returned for a second season fully aware that one good summer did not make him a world beater and fully determined to repay Middleton for their faith by producing even better form. With the bat he succeeded. Unfortunately, because the pitches were slower and the weather far from kind, his bowling was well below par and he had to be satisfied with a mere 31 wickets at the cost of more than 23 runs each to off-set a batting average of 59.61 culled from an aggregate of 1,073 runs – figures that falsely indicated he was a better batsman than Gary Sobers.

In his third season D'Oliveira was determined to restore some of the lustre that had been lost from his bowling. He succeeded by capturing 72 wickets at just over 15 runs each but had to settle for 678 runs and an average of 37.66 – figures denoting sound all-round cricket from a man who had now begun to think in terms of attempting another cricketing miracle. D'Oliveira was anxious to move up and sample first-class cricket in this country. Once again (and I do not think he ever knew it) I was instrumental in getting him an introduction to better cricket, for the late Ron Roberts, looking around for an all-rounder to complete a team he was taking to Rhodesia, had asked me if I knew of any such player in the leagues. I did not hesitate to suggest D'Oliveira was equal to the task. It was the beginning of a rapid rise to the top of the cricketing tree, and I have only one regret: I failed to persuade Lancashire to sign him. What was worse I failed even to persuade the county to send somebody to watch him in action. He was playing cricket regularly within a 20-mile radius of Old Trafford but not one Lancashire official was prepared to go and watch him, although by then he had earned a reputation for being a crowd-puller and a crowd-pleaser. Knowing his great desire to have a go in county cricket and of his friendship with Tom Graveney, a fellow member of the Ron Roberts touring team, I knew well that if Lancashire were not interested Worcestershire were.

Time and again I pleaded with those in power at Old Trafford to go and see for themselves the sort of player D'Oliveira was. Equally persistently they turned my appeals down and when both Worcestershire and Gloucestershire eventually made offers to D'Oliveira I decided to make one more attempt to bring the South African to Old Trafford. I asked him to delay his acceptance of the midland counties offers for one week. Alas it was no use. On the advice of two former England players, then committee members, but whose experience of D'Oliveira in action consisted of just one Sunday afternoon frolic in a benefit match they turned down the South African as 'just a Saturday afternoon slogger who could not be expected to make the grade'. They did not say this to the player himself. Diplomatically they wrote saying his engagement might be construed as a lack of opportunity for home-produced young cricketers but he knew, almost as well as I did, what the real reason was. And he was wise enough to keep it to himself.

The rest is cricketing history. Basil D'Oliveira made up a trio of Middleton recruits to Test cricket. Hedley Verity was the first. Then came Frank Tyson and finally D'Oliveira and, if it had not been for the second world war, Eric Denison might also have joined them. It is still a proud boast of Middleton Cricket Club that they helped three men on the way to cricketing glory. It could happen again, not necessarily at Middleton, but elsewhere in the Lancashire leagues for despite all the trials and tribulations which the clubs have to endure on the field and off and in face of ever rising costs the spirit is still high. One of these days there will come another Verity, another Tyson and, maybe, another D'Oliveira. It is part of the league cricket heritage that they should exist to provide opportunity for players, either professional or amateur, to climb the highest branches of the cricketing tree.

Chapter 13

A Representative Match Fit for Lord's

In those spells when rain stops play or prevents it starting it is an intriguing league cricket pastime to select two sides for a representative match to display all the skills and artistry of the Saturday afternoon game for the benefit of the pundits at either Old Trafford or Lord's. There is no lack of great players to form a panel for selection and it is an indication of the talent available from the professional ranks of the Lancashire and Central Lancashire Leagues alone when several international cricketers cannot be accommodated on one side or the other. Many have played in both leagues and using this as a basis for getting the best balance one can nominate two teams, always assuming the men chosen are at the peak of their form, who would provide cricketing entertainment of the highest possible order. Captaincy would, of course, play an important part and here the Central Lancashire League would have to look no further than the late Sir Frank Worrell.

Generally recognized as the most inspiring captain of recent years Worrell would have given his team a decided advantage for the Lancashire League, in which he never played except as a substitute professional on one or two occasions, would find the choice of their skipper much more difficult. Few of their professionals have had experience in the leadership line at the highest level like Worrell when he became the first coloured West Indies cricketer to lead a touring team both in this country and in Australia. But there is one man well versed in the arts of captaincy who can take charge of the Lancashire League eleven. His name is Bobby Simpson and he skippered Australia in England, in South Africa, in the West Indies and at home as well. On the strength of an en-

Edwin Kay (right) the most prolific amateur run-scorer in Central Lancashire League. With him, going out to open a Middleton innings, is Wally Hunt, a former Derbyshire batsman.

18. John Ikin, the former Lancashire and England left-hander, a great worker on and off the field for cricket in Staffordshire.

19. Action in the Bradford League—a Lidget Green batsman gets one through the slips in the match against Saltaire at Lidget Green.

A scene from the Staffordshire and South Cheshire League, with Porthill Park in opposition to Leek.

gagement with the Accrington club his choice cannot be opposed. Having named the captains let me now name their sides and discuss them in detail afterwards. My two teams would be:

Central Lancashire League:

    F. M. Worrell (Radcliffe and West Indies)
    C. J. Barnett (Rochdale and England)
    L. Warburton (Littleborough and Lancashire)
    G. S. Sobers (Radcliffe and West Indies)
    J. R. Reid (Heywood and New Zealand)
    C. G. Pepper (Rochdale and Australia)
    G. Tribe (Milnrow and Australia)
    W. Farrimond (Heywood and England)
    B. L. D'Oliveira (Middleton and England)
    H. Verity (Middleton and England)
    S. F. Barnes (Rochdale and England)
    12th man: Hanif Mohammad (Crompton and Pakistan).

Lancashire League:

    R. Simpson (Accrington and Australia)
    C. Hunte (Enfield and West Indies)
    E. Weekes (Bacup and West Indies)
    G. Headley (Haslingden and West Indies)
    L. N. Constantine (Nelson and West Indies)
    C. L. Walcott (Enfield and West Indies)
    V. Mankad (Haslingden and India)
    B. Dooland (East Lancashire and Australia)
    R. R. Lindwall (Nelson and Australia)
    G. A. R. Lock (Ramsbottom and England)
    F. H. Tyson (Todmorden and England)
    12th man: E. J. Barlow (Accrington and South Africa).

What a wealth of talent would be on parade if this 'dream' match were possible! Selection was difficult and there are so many good players overlooked. Sonny Ramadhin, for example, would have added spice to the Central Lancashire League attack but he was very much inferior in all-round ability to Cec Pepper at his best

G

and even such a superb left-hand spinner as Ellis Achong, who toured with the West Indies when Constantine was at his best, cannot be accommodated ahead of Hedley Verity or George Tribe. If the inclusion of Leslie Warburton may raise a few eyebrows let me say that this splendid cricketer would be no passenger in any side. He would, I feel sure, have played for England had Lancashire been able to break down his determination to stay in league cricket where for him there was security as well as satisfaction. I would be prepared to argue that he be given the new ball along with Sydney Barnes and in preference to Worrell or to Reid whose bowling with Heywood might well have been a revelation to those who saw him given few opportunities to get among the wickets for New Zealand.

The batting strength of both sides is tremendous. The Central Lancashire League could open with Worrell and Barnett, a happy choice. Both were handsome and powerful stroke players who seldom failed to profit from loose bowling. In addition each had a reputation for a willingness to attack and Barnett in particular was often a faster scorer than Wally Hammond for Gloucestershire and England. Sobers would fit in at No. 3 with distinction in this Central Lancashire League side and with Barnes the obvious No. 11 it really does not matter a great deal where the others batted. That would be the captain's headache. Tribe, Verity and Farrimond were all consistent scorers and with the choice of wicket-keepers admittedly very limited there can be little quibble at the choice of the Lancashire man who toured South Africa and won an England cap long before he was able to oust George Duckworth at Old Trafford. D'Oliveira wins a place because of his ability to rise to the big occasion. If there is a weakness in the side led by Worrell it would probably be the absence of a good off-spinner but with Verity, Tribe, Pepper and Sobers on hand the spin department would prove adequate, not to say a boon and blessing to the selectors of any World Eleven these days.

Turning to the Lancashire League side, what memories of exceptional pace and superb actions would be revived by the new ball pairing of Lindwall and Tyson who, at their very best, could have no peers in any generation of cricketers even if the real old-timers might cast their vote for Spofforth and Larwood! With Constantine to follow before the new ball's shine goes and Lock, Dooland and Mankad to provide the spin I doubt if Simpson would need to regard himself as a bowler at all. Behind the wicket there can surely be no questioning the right of Walcott to be classed as among the best of the few who have combined keeping with run-scoring power. This giant West Indies player could certainly team up with Hunte, Simpson, Weekes and Headley as the main batsmen in the side. All in all a match between the two chosen sides would provide cricket at its very best: attractive batsmanship, pace and spin in ideal bowling proportion and, of course, fielding of the highest possible order, with Constantine and Sobers the star performers. Should bad weather intervene there would be no lack of discussion groups to argue over the merits of the players, individually and collectively, but whether agreement on any one point would ever be reached is doubtful for cricket is such an unpredictable game! And therein lies its charm at all levels.

Chapter 14

League and County – Need for Better Relationship

Why, with all the talent that has been on display for the last 50 years or more, has Lancashire cricket not benefited more? The Lancashire leagues, with their determination to scour the world for professionals and their ability to bring them into regular contact with young amateurs, should provide a vast reservoir of potential cricketing talent for the county but most of Lancashire's recruits in recent years have come from the minor leagues where professionalism is modest and, in many instances, not practised. Yet nowhere else in England has the young cricketer a better chance to make progress than in the highly competitive leagues of Lancashire. It is a logical assumption, but it has seldom been proved right and by far the most prolific 'nursery' of Lancashire cricket in terms of recruits to Old Trafford and the county club is the Bolton League where there is seldom enough money to tempt the world-famous Test cricketer.

Looking no farther back than the first World War the Bolton League provided Lancashire with such players as Charlie Hallows, Dick Tyldesley, Dick Pollard, Bill Farrimond, Roy Tattersall and Len Wilkinson but in the same period the Lancashire League's contribution consisted of only two players who really made the top grade – Eddie Paynter and Winston Place – although there were others who by-passed Old Trafford to make their name elsewhere, including Dick Howorth and Eddie Cooper (Worcestershire) and Derek Shackleton (Hampshire). In the period between the two World Wars the Central Lancashire League, then at its best, could claim only two men of note in Frank Sibbles and Malcolm Taylor who went to Old Trafford and forced their way into the county side. Since the end of World War II the league's record has been better inasmuch as Malcolm Hilton, Peter Marner, Geoff Pullar, Jack Dyson and Geoff Clayton went to Old Trafford to win county caps, and Keith Andrew and Frank Tyson went to Northamptonshire to gain both county and Test caps.

These players apart it remains undeniable that Lancashire's principal source of supply has remained the smaller leagues. Brian Statham, for example, was a product of the North-Western League although he was actually playing with Stockport in the Central Lancashire League when first he came to Lancashire's attention. Jack Bond and Harry Pilling were also 'minor' league recruits despite their brief connections with Radcliffe and Oldham, and in the 1968 Lancashire County Eleven there was only one player recruited from the Lancashire League (David Lloyd from Accrington) and not one from the Central Lancashire sphere. All this provides ammunition for the critics of the leagues who maintain they are so wrapped up in their own affairs that the bigger world outside is of no concern to them. However, let me hasten to add that there is a friendly relationship between the Lancashire County Cricket Club and the leagues and always has been. That it could be developed into a much closer liason goes without saying and the sooner a very important barrier is breached the better it will be for cricket generally in Lancashire.

If the major leagues are inclined to go it alone and regard their own little cricketing world as the one that matters most, who can blame them? The Lancashire League caters for an area of some fifty square miles stretching from Accrington to Blackburn and Burnley and the Central Lancashire League, covering a slightly wider area from Stockport in Cheshire to Walsden on the border of Yorkshire, are independant and proud. They pay lip-service to Old Trafford but in reality have little in common with the county club. They turn to them only when accidents happen and a substitute professional is required although their officials are annually invited to Old Trafford for dinner and discussion aimed at securing a better relationship. There is good will on both sides but there is still a barrier of independence to be broken down. In Yorkshire every young cricketer has one ambition – to play for his county. In Lancashire, at least in many parts of the county, the ultimate aim of the young player appears to be to win a place in his local league side and bask in the glory of associating with world-class professionals. Often it is a passing phase and the good young cricketer, profiting from rubbing shoulders with the great ones, becomes the target for some minor league club who offer him attractive terms to turn professional on a match basis.

Here is extra money without risk. A Saturday afternoon professional can continue to do a job of work five days a week and make extra money on the sixth and seventh. Picking up £20 or £30 in this manner is a much more realistic approach to modern life than taking a chance on the ground-staff at Old Trafford where the wages until very recently seldom topped the £800 a year mark and the competition for places in the senior side is much fiercer and always, in addition, there is the prospect of looking for a job each winter. Spelt out in brief it is a question of security. In Yorkshire none of the leagues offer the sort of money to turn a youngster's attention from his natural desire to play for the county. There are, of course, occasional excursions over the border into Lancashire by a minority of young cricketers who cannot afford to await the invitation to Headingley or Bramall Lane but by and large York-shire's leagues work *for* the county. Lancashire's tend to work *against* the county.

Success, on the field and off it, is the natural desire of the Lancashire league clubs and if they come across a good young amateur there is no great desire to let the county know about him for the simple reason once he goes to Old Trafford he is lost to his local club. In Yorkshire where the county has no ground to maintain and no staff to employ the promising young player is 'netted and noted' by Arthur Mitchell and his coaching staff and allowed to return to his local club until an opportunity arises. In Lancashire the youngster of promise is watched and, if good enough, taken on to the staff. He becomes a professional immediately and is thus barred from playing with the club that has nursed him along. Nothing irks the league clubs more than to see a good boy who has left them for Old Trafford unemployed on a Saturday afternoon and yet unavailable to them. The leagues

themselves are partly to blame. Their rules are strict and rigidly
enforced and although several attempts have been made to revise
them and make it possible for Lancashire's staff players to continue to play as amateurs for their league club all have fallen down
because, it is argued with dour north country logic, a boy cannot
be a professional five days a week and an amateur on the other
two even if no payment is made to him!

Is it, then, any wonder that a good young player hesitates before
giving up the substance of league cricket for the shadow of the
first-class game? For the sake of all concerned and for cricket in
particular the leagues must relax their out-moded attitude to
professionalism until such time as their amateurs win a county cap
and become fully-fledged paid cricketers. On the other hand the
Lancashire County Cricket Club must make concessions. First of
all it must realize one plain basic fact. There is far more cricket
played outside of Old Trafford than inside it. And it is all Lancashire cricket. There are more youngsters playing cricket than
watching it at Old Trafford or elsewhere in the county and no club
has a wider choice than Lancashire. Yet their officials seldom go
out and about in the county and likewise the league and club
officials rarely visit the Red Rose headquarters. Invitations go
out to the 'top brass' for Test matches each year and token
appearances are made but this is merely scratching the surface of a
deep problem. Old Trafford should be 'home' to every cricket
club, large or small, in Lancashire.

The best-equipped cricket ground in the county could well be
the scene of the various league Cup Finals. I have advanced the
theory before, and taken it up with both parties, that Old Trafford
could be Lancashire's cricketing Wembley and in the often
golden days of September each league in its turn should parade its
gala occasion for the benefit of a far bigger cricketing population
than in their own immediate and intimate area. Once the ice is
broken the rest would follow. It may take time and it will certainly
call for a great deal of hard work and a lot of diplomatic discussions but there is nothing to stop Lancashire cricket producing
a real united front except the stubborness of those who control it.
Pride and a spirit of independence are admirable traits, but they

must not be carried too far. Cricket today acknowledges few barriers. Distance has been overcome and old prejudices broken down in common desire to pull together, yet in Lancashire there is still far too much parochialism with the leagues going their own sweet way and the county doing next to nothing about it. It is high time there was an end to this damaging isolationism.

What then is needed to bring about a new deal? Simply a man of integrity to bring the parties together and arbitrate on the tricky points at stake. At the moment it is mainly a question of who takes the initiative. Officials of the Lancashire County Cricket Club, realizing the great need for a better understanding, fear a snub. The leagues stay aloof because of a dread of losing their independence and progressive spirit and yet neither side has any real danger to face. There is room in plenty for both first-class cricket and league cricket in Lancashire. The county club seeks nothing more than a sincere and happy relationship and can offer much in the way of facilities, advice and possibly financial aid for the small clubs who fall upon hard times. For their part the leagues need fear no interference with their old-established customs and none in the furtherance of their own cricketing ideas and ideals. The basic need is for one to trust the other and work for the common good of cricket. Differences of opinion may well continue but, given good will and good mentors there is no real reason why county and league cricket in Lancashire should not be happily wed instead of diplomatically divorced.

Part II

Chapter 1

The Leagues in Detail: Lancashire and Cheshire

There can be no questioning the right of the Lancashire League in its claim to be the most powerful organization of its kind in the world. The league was formed in 1890 under the title of the North-East Lancashire Cricket League but adopted its present title two years later and has continued to play cricket without a break apart from the 1917 and 1918 seasons. The League survived a similar calamity in the Second World War when play proceeded throughout hostilities, although professionalism was abandoned, the amateurs held the fort providing much interesting cricket as well as producing evidence that there can be good cricket without professionals in any emergency.

The inaugural meeting of the League was held in Accrington on October 25, 1890 and the North-East Lancashire Cricket League was formed with thirteen clubs competing. They were: Burnley, Nelson, Colne, Bacup, Todmorden, East Lancashire, Enfield, Church, Haslingden, Ramsbottom, Lowerhouse, Accrington and Rawtenstall. Two weeks later, on November 8, 1890, Rishton was also admitted and these fourteen clubs still comprise the Lancashire League as it is today. Only one other club, Bury, has been privileged with membership and it joined in 1892 to fill the the place of Todmorden who withdrew on February 14, 1891, but returned to the fold in 1897 after Bury had enjoyed membership for two seasons before withdrawing in 1894. Down the years changes of officials and policy have been rare and it is the boast of the Lancashire League that throughout the whole of its 79 years there have been only four Honorary Secretaries. Jonathan Proctor, of Burnley, was the first and he took over in 1896 after one William Brown had been the paid organizer of the League from its conception in 1890 until, after six years of real hard work, he stood aside and left the responsibility of carrying on to what he jokingly but impressively termed the 'amateur' officials.

Mr Proctor remained in office for four seasons before, in 1900, handing over to William Barlow, J.P., a member of the Ramsbottom Club who continued in office for 35 years before making way for Gideon Holgate who, strangely enough, came from Clitheroe outside the League area. There are many in its sphere of activity who believe the Lancashire League owes its present unchallenged position to the splendid organising and diplomacy of Mr Barlow and most of the League's present strict rules and regulations were prepared and enforced by him. But when he stepped down and Mr Holgate took his place the Lancashire League continued to maintain and enhance its reputation. Such was Mr Holgate's talents as a cricket administrator that the Lancashire County Cricket Club co-opted him as a member of the Old Trafford Club Committee and came to rely upon him as the man who would strive to ensure a better relationship between the county and the leagues.

Mr Holgate continued in office until 1950 when ill-health forced him to hand over to Jack Isherwood, of the Accrington Club, who is still maintaining the League's reputation of enjoying the services of top-class administrators in an honorary capacity. Mr Isherwood served his apprenticeship as Mr Holgate's assistant for five years and he, in his turn, has been blessed with excellent unpaid assistants in Mr D. George (Accrington) from 1950 until 1955, Mr J. Cruise (Clayton-le-Moors) from 1955 to 1966 and since then by Mr W. L. Eastwood of the Burnley Cricket Club. Eleven men have enjoyed the honour of being President of the Lancashire Cricket League and the first of them, way back in the foundation year of 1890, was Mr James Sutcliffe, of Burnley, a man of immense stature in the county's sporting spheres. He remained at the head of affairs until 1898 when Mr John Trego Gill of Ramsbottom took over and stayed until 1905 when he vacated the office in favour of another redoubtable Ramsbottom man, one Dr Crawshaw, J.P. The doctor remained in charge until 1921 when he stood aside for Mr E. Crabtree of Lytham who took office for a spell of 25 years –

the longest single term tenure of a League President. It was under Mr Crabtree's influence, from 1921 until 1946, that the Lancashire League built up its reputation for scouring the cricketing world for its professionals.

Mr H. Longworth (Rawtenstall) succeeded Mr Crabtree, in 1946 and was President until 1954 when he handed over to Mr H. Sutcliffe, of Todmorden, who in turn gave way to Mr H. Foster (Ramsbottom) in 1958. Then in 1959 came Mr J. Ashworth (Accrington) and in 1961 Mr J. G. Crabtree, of Burnley, stepped up for two years before giving way to Mr A. King, J.P. (Todmorden) who served until 1965 when Mr C. R. Davies, T.D., J.P., of East Lancashire Cricket Club, took over after serving as the League Chairman since 1955 and being a prominent amateur batsman with the East Lancashire Club. The League runs divisions for first and second elevens as well as a most successful Knock-out Competition for the Worsley Cup and rightly considers its rules and regulations must be strictly and impartially applied to maintain the League's reputation for fair play. In the main its cricket is played under MCC rules although the eight-ball over has been found a successful deviation from English custom. Rigid control of professionalism is maintained by a series of rules demanding their appearance in every League and Cup match unless incapacitated, and forbidding their appearance elsewhere, without the permission of the club committee on a specified number of occasions each summer. The League also insists on the standardization of the professionals' playing contract in certain details although, of course, it does not lay down any limits as to payment or length of service.

Its amateur players have to fulfil strict qualifications, either by birth or genuine residence within two miles' radius of the boundary of the club for whom he wishes to play. Certain privileges are allowable; for instance, a cricketer who has spent the whole of his youth from the age of 14 to 21, shall be deemed to have qualified for a club within the two mile limit, and a man with a genuine business address for at least twelve months may also be permitted to play in the Lancashire League. These restrictions are regarded as irksome in many cases but the League rigidly adheres to them believing it is better to move cautiously towards what many in the League believe to be still more progress. When the League was first formed professionalism was permissable and encouraged with each club allowed, if it so chose, to employ two paid players. It is beyond argument that the basis of their engagement was primarily as coaches or groundsmen with the ability to produce a few runs and a few wickets in matches when the club amateurs were in trouble. Nowadays, and for many years past, a club is limited to one professional and it is inevitable that these paid players, recruited in recent years from far and wide, should produce figures that dominate the League's record book.

The highest innings yet played in a Lancashire League match is the 195 not out hit by Everton Weekes, for Bacup against Enfield in 1949, but the late Collie Smith, another grand West Indies cricketer, hit up a magnificent 306 not out for Burnley in a Worsley Cup clash against Lowerhouse in the 1959 season; but for sheer batting consistency the performance of the Australian Bill Alley, who hit over a thousand runs in five successive seasons at Colne beginning in 1948 will take some beating. Alley's exact tally was 5,713 runs and for weeks at a time he had an average of three-figure proportions. Nonetheless the indefatigable Weekes, in six seasons with Bacup, albeit not in succession, collected some 8,036 runs for an average of 91.32 and was the first batsman in the League in each of those 'golden' summers to reach 1,000 runs. Weekes holds the record for the highest ever batting average in the Lancashire League – a fabulous 158.25 from an aggregate of 1,256 runs; and the most runs ever hit in any one summer in the League also stands to the credit of Weekes, who, in the 1951 season at Bacup rattled up 1,518 runs – more than a hundred better than the next best until in 1959 Australian captain Bobby Simpson reached 1,444 on behalf of Accrington. From the bowling point of view the most devastating attacker in the history of the Lancashire League was the West Indies fast bowler Charlie Griffith who, in 1964, captured 144 wickets for Burnley at a cost of only 5.20 runs per victim. His tremendous impact upon the opposing batsman was such that Burnley not only won the League championship but also collected a record aggregate number of points – 70.

Griffith takes pride of place by just one wicket and one has to go back to 1900 to find a bowler with similar destructiveness when Jack Usher, the Haslingden professional, captured 143 wickets at 6.03 each. But for the really unplayable match return I must recall the power and majesty of Learie Constantine who took all ten Accrington wickets for only ten runs on a glorious May afternoon in 1934 when at the height of his powers with Nelson. The details of the Accrington innings reveal that Constantine conceded 10 out of the 12 runs scored in producing an analysis of 6.1 – 1 – 10 – 10, whilst, at the other end, the ever reliable Alf Pollard had figures of 6 – 5 – 1 – 0. It is true a story that two old-timers on the Nelson pavilion side, in discussing the merit of the two returns, sadly agreed 'Connie were a bit expensive–weren't he'.

Previously Ted MacDonald, the Australian and Lancashire fast bowler, also playing for Nelson, had taken all ten Burnley wickets for 18 runs in 1923 only to yield his record a year later to Fred Hartley, a canny local-born left-hand spinner who played several times for Lancashire and on May 17, 1924, claimed all ten Ramsbottom wickets for 16 runs on behalf of the Bacup Club. In point of fact, capturing all ten wickets is not particularly unusual in league cricket and the Lancashire League alone records some 15 occasions.

Hat-tricks, too, are not infrequent but in 1930 Jimmy Boon, the Burnley professional, recorded the only 'double' in the League's history by taking six wickets in six deliveries against Rawtenstall. George Macaulay, the former Yorkshire and England bowler, playing for Todmorden in 1938 three times recorded hat-tricks and once took four wickets in five deliveries. He also took nine wickets for ten runs in a Worsley Cup final against Ramsbottom. In Cup matches alone that season Macaulay picked up 17 wickets at the ridiculous price of only 3.41 runs each. Talking of hat-tricks one must not overlook the amateurs and when in 1961 Roger Sharp, of East Lancashire, dismissed three batsmen with successive deliveries in successive matches, against Burnley at Blackburn on August 19 and in the return match at Burnley on August 26 there was a frenzied rush to turn up the records and see if this was a feat unparalleled in the Lancashire League. One cannot blame Burnley supporters for failing to acknowledge anything better.

For sheer consistency there are none to compare with the old-timer Vic Norbury who in his sojourn with the East Lancashire Club captured over 1,000 wickets and paid less than ten runs each for them. In this respect the name of Fred Hartley crops up yet again for this ever-accurate left-handed spinner topped the 100 wicket mark in three successive seasons for Church – in 1947–9. But perhaps the most impressive afternoon's work with the ball stands to the credit of Subash Gupte, the Indian leg-spinner, who was professional at Rishton on Whit Tuesday, 1956, when he claimed eight wickets for 19 runs and twice performed the hat-trick against Accrington. Professionals seldom stayed long enough to produce the consistent bowling returns of some of the Lancashire League amateurs and there are several unpaid attackers with more than a thousand victims to their credit. Pride of place in this amateur roll of honour must go to Fred Duerr who, in the course of a 28-year career in the League claimed more than 2,000 League and Worsley Cup wickets. Duerr started his trail of destruction with Bacup in 1902 and when he left to join Rams-bottom in 1907 he had taken some 335 wickets for 3,903 runs in League matches alone. He went on to perform even greater feats with his new club and from 1908 to 1929 a total of 1,620 batsmen fell to his guile and canny control over length at a cost of just over 15 runs each, although his overall 'payment' was 10.11 per victim in League matches. Throw in the Worsley Cup successes and Duerr's record bears comparison with the best in any sphere. Three times he topped the 100 wickets-a-season mark and so, too, did Alf Pollard of whom Learie Constantine once said that he never saw him bowl a long hop or a full toss.

Pollard, in nineteen seasons with Nelson and Colne, took 1,390 wickets averaging 79 victims for each-and-every season he was sending down his medium-paced seamers although, of course, in his day the term had not been coined. Pollard's best season was undoubtedly in 1919 when on behalf of Nelson he dismissed 112 batsmen for 7.74 runs each but he was often heard to recall a more memorable occasion for him when as a veteran approaching retirement in 1934 he bowled throughout an Accrington innings against Nelson conceding only one run – and that off the bat edge. A real

21. Jimmy Hyde, the free-scoring Middleton left-hander, in action in the Central Lancashire League.

22. Frank Tyson, a Middleton and Central Lancashire League recruit to England and Northamptonshire cricket.

23. Basil D'Oliveira (centre), the Worcestershire and England all-rounder, returns to Middleton to celebrate his success with former Central Lancashire League colleagues.

cricketing artist was Pollard and another old-timer who made his mark in the League was Billy Fenwick, of Ramsbottom, who in 1900 became the first amateur to take 100 wickets in a season. His figures of 137 wickets at a cost of 7.27 runs each is still the League record for an unpaid bowler and Fenwick was one of the 'old brigade' who did much to launch the Lancashire League on its way to success and domination of the Saturday afternoon cricketing sphere. Coming back to more recent times the League can boast few amateur bowlers of the Fenwick-Duerr-Pollard class but occasionally, in the face of much fiercer professional competition the young amateurs do steal the headlines and the thunder.

Few made such an impressive debut in the League as Nelson's Roy Pickles who, given his baptism against Burnley in 1943, took five wickets for only seven runs and threw in a hat-trick for good measure. The ball with which Pickles performed the feat was afterwards mounted and presented to him. An even better performance came from a youngster of sixteen, still at school, when, in 1947, Tommy Dickinson playing for East Lancashire against Colne, dismissed six batsmen for only nine runs and hit the stumps each time. A fast bowler of exceptional promise Dickinson played several games for Lancashire but declined to become a professional and eventually settled in the South of England where he combined school teaching with impressive performances in club cricket. A year later, in 1948, Colin Maden, a Burnley amateur, took eight Haslingden wickets for six runs and hit the stumps six times in the process, whilst in 1950 Steve Wells, of Rawtenstall, grabbed four Enfield wickets with successive deliveries in an over-all return of 7 – 2 – 11 – 7. Professionals cannot expect to be the bosses all the time!

Turning to the amateur batsmen in the Lancashire League it is pleasing to record that two players, George Parker, of Haslingden, and James Midgeley, of Bacup, have topped the 1,000 runs in a season mark. Parker achieved the feat in 1908 when he hit 1,013 runs for an average of 48.24 and was awarded a gold medal; Midgeley in 1929 hit 1,130 runs for Bacup at an average of 70.62 but there is no record of him also being awarded a medal to mark a rare cricketing performance. The League's list of meritorious

H

batting performances singles out more than a dozen amateur batsmen who have hit half-centuries on every ground in the League and one of them was Chick Hawkwood, of Nelson, whom Constantine regarded as probably the best amateur batsman he played with or against in the Lancashire League. But it was after Constantine had moved on in 1948 that Hawkwood and his partner, Clarry Winslow, set up a Nelson club record with an opening partnership unbroken at 198 when Burnley were beaten at Turf Moor. Hawkwood's share was 105 and Winslow contributed 87. Another prolific partnership standing out in the records recalls the man the Lancashire League rightly regards as their most successful contribution to first-class cricket for in 1949 Eddie Paynter, who hit 125 not out, and his professional colleague, Des Fothergill, put together a fourth wicket partnership worth 248 for Enfield against Colne.

Fothergill contributed 166 to a partnership which is still the League's joint highest-ever and the match produced a record aggregate of 503 runs in five hours of top-class cricketing entertainment with Enfield declaring at 309 – 4 and Colne replying with 194 – 5. Another all-amateur partnership of considerable merit was the first wicket stand of 196 for Todmorden against Accrington in 1947 when Walter Scott and Arthur Cunliffe hit up 196 before Scott was dismissed for 81 and Cunliffe stayed unbeaten for 102. In 1952 Eric Denison, the Todmorden professional, and Harold Dawson, an amateur colleague, did even better when they put together a second wicket partnership worth 214 runs with Denison compiling 103 and Dawson 104 and both going in unbeaten. It was also Todmorden amateur, John Crowther, who achieved Worsley Cup fame in 1938 by scoring 144 runs and taking five wickets for 32 runs in the final tie against Haslingden played at Burnley in 1938. Bacup also lay claim to several splendid partnerships and in 1954 at Colne Everton Weekes, the club professional, and Stan Entwistle, his amateur partner, equalled the Fothergill-Paynter record of 248 for Enfield which they put together in a second wicket stand of 111 minutes to win a memorable game against a keen Colne attack and the clock.

Nelson are the only Lancashire League club to win the League

INNINGS OF EAST LANCASHIRE

PLAYED AT

RAMSBOTTOM, APRIL 14th, 1900.

F. MOSLEY	Caught and Bowled Taylor	0
F. R. CARMICHAEL	Bowled Fenwick	0
R. C. DICKINSON	L.B.W. bowled Fenwick	0
A. SCOTT	Stumped Barlow, bowled Fenwick	2
WOODLEY	Bowled Fenwick	0
R. HARGREAVES	Run out	1
W. H. NUTTALL	Bowled Fenwick	0
J. W. CARMICHAEL	Caught Fenwick, bowled Taylor	1
D. R. GRADWELL	Caught Berry, bowled Fenwick	3
J. SMITH	L.B.W., bowled Fenwick	1
W. HOWARD	Not out	0
	TOTAL INNINGS	8

RUNS AT THE FALL OF EACH WICKET.

1 for 0 : 2 for 0 : 3 for 0 : 4 for 2 : 5 for 3 : 6 for 3 : 7 for 4 : 8 for 7 : 9 for 8 : 10 for 8.

BOWLERS' NAMES	Total Overs	Total Maiden Overs	Total Runs	Total Wickets
TAYLOR	9	6	5	2
FENWICK	9	6	3	7

INNINGS OF RAMSBOTTOM

PLAYED AT

RAMSBOTTOM, APRIL 14th, 1900.

A. J. SCOWSILL	Caught Dickinson, bowled Woodley	0
S. ROBERTS	Caught F. Carmichael, bowled J. W. Carmichael	2
TAYLOR	L.B.W., bowled Woodley	0
J. LEACH	Bowled Woodley	24
A. BERRY	Run out	2
J. HAYDOCK	Caught Mosley, bowled Howarth	4
W. GORTON	Not out	1
W. B. SADLER	Bowled Howard	4
J. HAWORTH	Caught Scott, bowled Howard	0
W. FENWICK	Caught Scott, bowled Howard	0
J. BARLOW	Absent	0
	Extras	8
	TOTAL INNINGS	45

RUNS AT THE FALL OF EACH WICKET.

1 for 4 : 2 for 5 : 3 for 5 : 4 for 20 : 5 for 37 : 6 for 37 : 7 for 45 : 8 for 45 : 9 for 45 : 10 for 45.

BOWLERS' NAMES	Total Overs	Total Maiden Overs	Total Runs	Total Wickets
WOODLEY	14	10	14	3
J. W. CARMICHAEL	7	1	16	1
NUTTALL	3	2	2	0
HOWARD	3.4	1	5	4

championship in four successive seasons, 1934–7 when, of course, Constantine was the club professional and the side drew record crowds wherever they went. Burnley and Accrington each claim a hat-trick of championship successes, both in the distant past, with Burnley succeeding in 1906–8 and Accrington in the war years, 1914–16 when all-amateur cricket was the rule. Looking at the championship distinction from the overall point of view, Nelson take the major honours with sixteen senior titles to their credit and East Lancashire take pride of place in the Worsley Cup with nine successes since the competition was first introduced in 1919. Colne were the inaugural winners of a trophy that produced record gate receipts of £713 in 1964 when the Burnley-Rishton clash drew the biggest-ever crowd. Proud of its past, confident of its future, the Lancashire League continues to provide a class of cricket unique inasmuch as it gives the local boy a chance to rub shoulders with international cricketers from all over the world

Chapter 2

The Central Lancashire League

Like the Lancashire League, the Central Lancashire League also saw the first light of day in 1892 and down the years it has done much to provide a similar kind of cricketing entertainment in a wider area bounded by Stockport on the Cheshire side, and Walsden on the verge of Yorkshire, taking in the cotton towns of Oldham, Rochdale, Ashton, Radcliffe, Heywood and Middleton and incorporating the smaller districts of Royton, Werneth, Littleborough, Castleton Moor, Crompton and Milnrow. Bury were foundation members of the League and also members at one time or another were Darwen, Dukinfield, Glossop, Longsight, Moorside, Stalybridge and Todmorden. There were nine clubs in the league in 1892 and it was not until 1907 that the present complement of fourteen was reached and even then there were resignations and withdrawals because of a lack of facilities or support, and from 1916 until 1936 the Central Lancashire League again reverted to a twelve-club competition. Stockport and Radcliffe were then taken within the fold and the formation has remained unbroken ever since although suggestions have been put forward from time to time for an expansion that would see the formation of two divisions with promotion and relegation issues.

Realizing the need for introducing a greater element of competition I took a leading part, when Honorary Secretary of the League from 1943 to 1959, in attempting to bring about such a change but the clubs could not be persuaded. Some, of course, were in favour but the League rules, which have stood the test of time, insist on a two-third's majority being necessary before any rule can be changed. This was never forthcoming and the chief argument against expansion was the view of the smaller clubs in the league that 'something bigger is not always better'. It was a belief un-provable until the scheme had been put into practice and whilst there were frequent applications for membership from other clubs in other leagues the issue was always side-stepped. Who can say whether such a new look to league cricket as envisaged with a bigger and wider-spread league with two divisions and consequent battles for promotion and against relegation would have attracted public attention to any higher degree? Certainly crowd figures in recent summers have been disappointing but the weather has not been kind and without sunshine cricket at any level is not the ideal Saturday or Sunday afternoon entertainment. But there is evidence still of a great pulling power whenever there is some-thing a little different on the league cricketing 'menu' and the Central Lancashire League has attracted far bigger crowds to watch its Rothman Cup matches than it has for its domestic league or Wood Cup matches.

Here, to my way of thinking, is an indication that a further exploration of the two division plan might well be worthwhile, for winter after winter the club balance sheets reveal that cricket by itself cannot be made a paying proposition and if it were not for the sidelines of bigger and better bars, more luxurious social sections, and the stepping up of the 'pools,' money would indeed be scarce. I am told, however, this was always the case and possibly always will be. The Central Lancashire League, like the Lancashire League, has been fortunate in the choice of its officials and the League's first President was the Reverend J. R. Napier, vicar of Walsden and a prominent public schools cricketer of his day when he played for Marlborough and Lancashire. The Reverend Napier played a prominent part in the foundation of the League which began as the South-East Lancashire League but changed after one year to its present title and the 'sporting parson' remained in office until the end of the 1894 season when he stepped down, confident that all was going well, in favour of Mr W. Thompson, an Oldham man of considerable sporting influence in his day. Nonetheless, Rev. Napier remained a keen supporter of the Central Lancashire League in general and the Walsden club in particular for many years and an old minute book reveals that several times he needed no second bidding to come to the financial aid of one or two clubs who found cricket an expensive and laborious luxury even in the easy-going days at the turn of the century.

After Mr Thompson, who held office until 1900, came another famous cricketing name to lend distinction to the Central Lancashire League for in stepped Mr S. Hill-Wood, a member of an illustrious Glossop family who provided Derbyshire with both players and officials of distinction for a great many years. When, in 1907, Mr Hill-Wood stood down his place was taken by Mr A. Clegg but he served for one year only before stepping aside for the man who was to become the League's greatest benefactor – Alderman John Henry Wood, a Mayor of Middleton, a captain of the local club, and the donor in 1921 of the League's trophy for a knock-out competition which he saw won first, fittingly enough, by his own club, Middleton, after a thrilling tied final with Littleborough at Heywood. Alderman Wood remained in office from 1913 until 1926 – a long term for any President – steadily steering the League through the difficult days of the first World War and guiding it back to peace-time standards and ideals when hostilities ceased. Again early minute books reveal the generosity as well as the sportsmanship of a 'Grand Old Man' of league cricket. His name is honoured throughout the Central Lancashire League and even when, in his old age, he was no longer able to play a practical role, either for the league or for his club, the Alderman was always available for consultation and advice. There are people living in Middleton today who still speak with awe of the mourners that gathered for the Alderman's funeral. 'They came from far and near, the wealthy in their top hats and frock coats, the poor in their cloth caps and mufflers, and there were tears in the eyes of hundreds who lined the route as well as amongst those who walked in sympathy behind the funeral procession,' says one old-timer who had played cricket and worked for Alderman Wood throughout his sporting life.

He was succeeded in office by Mr A. Cummings but in the 1930s the League changed its policy in regard to its figureheads and Presidents were elected for two-year terms in the belief the greatest cricketing honour the League had to offer should go round and many are the worthy names that have graced the list since the days of Alderman John Henry Wood. Several of them, like the old Middleton stalwart, were players before they became officials and one, in particular, Arthur L. Taylor from the Ashton Cricket Club, was still a player when he was elected League President in 1938 and 1939, and so, too, was his successor, Mr Frank Hargreaves, of the Rochdale Cricket Club, who took office just as war broke out. Nonetheless Mr Hargreaves, like Alderman Wood in the first World War, led the way in keeping the League functioning. To this day the President of the League is a 'working' official, attending and taking control of the monthly meetings of the League Committee, a body formed by two representatives from each competing club permitted one vote on all matters. In addition the League appoints a chairman to learn the ropes before stepping up into the higher office and by and large the system works well.

Six men have served as Honorary Secretaries, a job which demands tremendous enthusiasm as well as administrative ability, and the doyen of the six was undoubtedly Mr 'Dicky' Thompson, of Oldham, who held office from 1917 until 1934 and retired to contribute an even greater service to his second love – Rugby League football. The League's first honorary secretary was Mr J. G. Prizeman who was elected at an explorative meeting in the autumn of 1891 and took over on the formation of the League a year later to serve until 1915 when he stood aside for Mr J. A. Hincliffe. Then came Mr Thompson and, succeeding him, Mr J. Cummings of the Werneth Cricket Club, son of a former President, who remained in office until 1942 when military service took him out of the district and enabled me to step in and help repay league cricket for the happy years and countless friends made on the field of play. In 1959 pressure of business reluctantly forced me to step aside in favour of my twin brother, Edwin, who had been assistant secretary doing a great deal of hard work for five years and continuing in office until the present time. Edwin Kay must be the only League Cricket secretary who has scored more than 10,000 runs before taking office, but many of his present colleagues on the League Committee were also good players in their day.

Surely this is a good sign. When men are prepared to pay for the good days on the field with tremendous effort in committee in later years there is much to be said for the game of cricket as a breeder of character and goodwill. One of the weaknesses of the Central Lancashire League, alas, has been its reluctance to keep records. Unlike the Lancashire League it does not now list great performances in its League Handbook. Nor does it acknowledge any performance, however outstanding, as a 'record'. It merely asserted until a few years ago that when in 1951 Frank Worrell, who was professional with Radcliffe, hit 1,694 runs it was an 'outstanding achievement', better than the 1,501 Worrell had hit in 1949 and also improving upon the 1,466 runs made by Vinoo Mankad of India and Castleton Moor a year or so earlier. The League handbook did, at one time, refer to another splendid achievement by Vijay Manjrekar, also of India, who in his first season with Castleton Moor in 1956 hit 1,456 runs and was deprived by bad weather of several innings in August when he would undoubtedly have passed Worrell's remarkable tally.

Today all references to outstanding individual performances by both amateur and professional batsmen and bowlers have been deleted from the official handbook and I have had to refer to older volumes to discover some of the splendid performances in a sphere of cricket that can ill afford to neglect the statistical side of its fine history. I discovered that when Leslie Warburton hit 1,385 runs as the Littleborough professional in 1937 he was probably the first Central Lancashire League batsman to top the four figure aggregate although many old-timers insist that, way back in the early days of the century, George Radcliffe, of Stalybridge, with the aid of several friendly fixtures, scored more than 1,000 runs and earned a reputation for being a 'difficult man to dismiss'. How naive but how typical of league cricket! Eric Denison (Middleton), Jock Livingston (Royton), Cec Pepper (Rochdale), John Reid (Heywood), Charles Barnett (Rochdale) and, of course, Garfield Sobers (Radcliffe) are other professionals to top 1,000 runs in later years but I have yet to hear of any amateur other than Middleton's J. M. Hyde doing the same. In the 1955 season Hyde hit 1,056 runs for an average of 45.91 in what was a memorable season for a stylish left-hander who, like his then opening partner, Edwin Kay, also accomplished the rare feat of topping a career figure of 10,000 runs and recording at least one half-century on each ground in the League.

From the bowling point of view Dhatu Phadkar, the Indian Test fast bowler, who played for Rochdale in 1955 and took 154 wickets, must have been the most deadly attacker the League has known although it is on the records at Milnrow that in 1949 George Tribe, the Australian left-hander who later played with distinction for Northamptonshire, took 148 wickets and suffered badly from indifferent fielding. George Pope, the old Derbyshire seam bowler, broke all Heywood Cricket Club records in the same year with a haul of 148 victims at less than 10 runs each but he could not match the all-round brilliance of a later Heywood professional, John Reid who, in his first season at The Crimble, scored over 1,000 runs and took more than 100 wickets to share with such great players as Phadkar, Barnett, Mankad, Worrell, Sobers and Warburton the distinction of producing the 'double'. Individual batting performances of outstanding merit are numerous and without claiming 'records' on behalf of any it is interesting to point out that in 1915 Harry Smith, a rotund little amateur with Walsden, hit 215 not out against Moorside one sunny Saturday afternoon and followed up a week later in the return match by hitting 119. The first encounter between these two clubs that summer saw Walsden reach a total of 340 and Moorside were beaten although answering with 277. Surely there can seldom have been more runs scored in a five-hour league cricket match? There must have been some revealing bowling figures then as undoubtedly there were years later when, at Middleton in 1952, Frank Worrell and Billy Greenhalgh of Radcliffe put together an unfinished opening partnership of 303 with Worrell reaching 152 and Greenhalgh 144 before a declaration was made – after two and three-quarter hours at the crease.

Only a few weeks earlier the Middleton professional, Eric Price, who had previously played for the Moonrakers as an amateur and gone on to play with Lancashire and Essex, had taken all ten Littleborough wickets for just four runs! One year later an amateur, Tom Everett of Oldham, also captured all ten wickets but it is not stated at what cost – another sad lapse of a league that is not very record conscious. But for sheer bowling deadliness what about the magnificent Wood Cup return of a burly Australian pace bowler, Bill Cockburn, who succeeded George Tribe at Milnrow, and in 1953 captured nine Heywood wickets for 16 runs in less than an hour in a match his side won in a night's cricket lasting less than 2¼ hours? Talking about the Wood Cup the Middleton Cricket Club can lay claim to a couple of meritorious performances even if they were not records. In the 1948 season Edwin Kay batted throughout the competition before losing his wicket for the first time in the final tie when, happily enough, the blow was softened by victory for his side over Oldham. Years before, in 1936, Tom Jacques, a Towncroft off-spinner with a near-perfect bowling action, had taken 8 Rochdale wickets for 40 runs in a winning final for the Middletonians but later this remarkable return by an amateur faded into the second best category when Jack Olive (Radcliffe) claimed 9 – 40 against Oldham in 1943. Nonetheless for sheer destructiveness the Wood Cup finals have brought no greater devastation than the 7 – 7 figures of Bryn Howells, for Milnrow against Werneth in 1939, when the Cup was won and lost in one night.

The official League Handbook does provide, however, a list of honours winners from the team point of view and pride of place for senior championships won goes to the Rochdale Cricket Club who have nineteen times finished top in the league table. Littleborough come next with ten winning championships and Middleton have been champions seven times. Heywood, winners in both 1967 and 1968 have now taken major honours eight times to suggest that some of the leeway between Rochdale and their rivals is being made up but it will be a long time yet before Rochdale yield pride of place in the Central Lancashire League. Added to their championship successes have been ten Wood Cup victories with Werneth challenging by winning the Knock-out Competition on eight occasions and Middleton recording a similar number of Cup victories. Three times – in 1949 when Stockport and Milnrow shared honours; in 1962 when Walsden and Stockport could not be separated; and in 1965 when Crompton and Stockport finished level – have senior championships been shared. In 1944 Stockport and Oldham shared the Second Division title and in this sphere of second team cricket Middleton top the honours list with fourteen championships to their name. In addition the League presents two trophies, the Whittaker Cups, for competition amongst Third Elevens and in this junior competition the League is split into two sections in a effort to curtail travelling for matches played in the evenings.

The arguments abound as to the respective merits of the Lancashire and Central Lancashire Leagues, but from the administrative point of view I have no doubt at all that the Lancashire League sets the near-perfect example of both control and conduct; however when it comes to the playing sides there can be no real answer to a cricketing argument that has been waging ever since the leagues' birth in 1892. Amateurs who have played in both spheres tend to vote the Lancashire League the superior of the two because of its more telling professional policy but the paid players who have held engagements in both spheres are hard pressed to nominate the better. They sometimes stress that the pitches are often just that shade better in the Lancashire League and this, of course, must have an effect on the standard of the game but by and large there is no general agreement on the quality of the cricket played. It is best to agree to differ!

Yet this cannot be done without paying attention to the many other leagues, not only of those in Lancashire but also of those in Yorkshire and in the Midlands as well as the North-East and Scotland. He would be a very bold man indeed who would nominate any one league the 'best' for in Lancashire alone there are over thirty well established leagues, ranging from the powerful ones where professionalism is practised to the little but equally enthusiastic amateur organizations where facilities for play are often the biggest handicap to be overcome. The Lancashire Cricket Annual, edited year after year and often at some personal expense by Albert E. Hall, of Bolton, lists them all.

Chapter 3

The Bolton League

Young in years but old in its ways the Bolton League was formed as an off-shoot of the older-established Bolton and District Cricket Association as recently as 1930. Only in the manner of its more modest approach to professionalism does the League fail to rank with the Central Lancashire League and the Lancashire League. In one respect, as has been mentioned before, the Bolton League has the edge over every other cricketing organization for it has been a most prolific nursery for the Lancashire County Cricket Club. The Bolton area has produced some magnificent cricketers including the famous Tyldesley brothers, Harry, James, William and Richard, but not, of course, the even more redoubtable Johnny and Ernest, who were products of the Worsley district and learned the game in the Manchester and District Cricket Association, a cricketing body embracing all-amateur clubs in all parts of Lancashire. Charlie Hallows, Bill Farrimond, Dick Pollard, Len Wilkinson and Roy Tattersall were more recent recruits to Old Trafford and all, along with many more, learned to play cricket in the Bolton area.

Ten clubs, Astley Bridge, Bradshaw, Egerton, Farnworth, Heaton, Kearsley, Little Lever, Tonge, Walkden and Westhoughton, were founder members of the League and in 1936 Eagley and Horwich RMI were enrolled. At one time Radcliffe were also members of a League which covers a crowded six-mile area from the Bolton Town Hall and provides the sort of cricket that is never without 'local derby' atmosphere. From the administrative point of view each club nominates one representative annually to serve on the League Committee and these men are augmented by four 'officials', a President, Chairman, Honorary

Treasurer and Honorary Secretary plus three specially co-opted members chosen for their local knowledge and cricketing background. It is on record that at one time the Bolton League also appointed an Honorary Solicitor and expected him to attend the monthly meetings. One is tempted to ponder if his main duty was to 'umpire' on the many knotty points that must arise from such a crowded and enthusiastic gathering of cricket lovers.

In addition to its First and Second Division championships the League also enjoys its Hamer Cup Competition, a knock-out tournament that used to highlight the many pleasant summer evenings in the area but is now one of the many Sunday cricketing attractions in and around Bolton. With the senior championship goes the Warburton Cup and the second elevens take the Howarth Cup when topping the table. It is a measure of the soundness of the League that no one club can claim a monopoly of championships or Hamer Cup successes. Farnworth are usually round and about when the honours are being handed out but they are not so very far in front of their fellow clubs and in a couple of years or so the balance could easily be adjusted. Time limit cricket tends to restrict high scoring but there have been many fine performances at both club and individual level to highlight the years before and after World War II. It would be hard to find a better Saturday afternoon total under limited playing conditions than the 269 – 5 hit up by Heaton against Walkden in 1932 or, looking in the other direction, difficult to pinpoint one more depressing than the mere 11 runs Egerton claimed when their last man was dismissed against a lively Little Lever attack in 1957. In Cup games, always played to a conclusion, it is easier to trace bigger and better totals than are possible in restricted League clashes and before they left the League to join the Central Lancashire organization Radcliffe made their mark with a grand 309 tally against Westhoughton in 1935. Strange to relate, the same total was achieved by Farnworth against Bradshaw in 1940, during the 'phony' war period.

On the other hand the Hamer Cup has produced no greater disaster than the total of 19 put together somewhat disjointedly by the Egerton batsmen against Tonge in 1948 but turning to the individuals there must have been some memorable cricket when Harold Catterall of Eagley hit up a superb 139 not out against Heaton in 1954 – an innings still ranking as a record in the Hamer Cup Competition. It is doubtful, however, if the Bolton League ever had a more prolific scorer than the West Indian, Ken Rickards, who holds both the individual and the aggregate batting records in the league's history. In 1955 Rickards hit a superb 156 for Farnworth against Tonge and in the same season the West Indian batsman, a stylist as well as a punishing stroke-player, returned a total of 1,389 runs in League and Cup matches. In restricted League games he compiled 1,238 of the runs and it will be a long time before Rickard's achievements, including eight centuries hit in one season, are forgotten by the spectators or surpassed by other players. Two cricketers of international repute, Cecil Parkin (Tonge) and Vinoo Mankad, playing professionally for the same club, share the bowling record for League matches when in 1932 Parkin took 110 wickets and, in 1961, Mankad equalled that number but the over-all record in League and Cup matches stands to the credit of a local-born professional, Fred Hartley who, in addition to playing Bolton League cricket, also shone in the more exalted company of the Lancashire and Central Lancashire Leagues as well as turning out far too infrequently for Lancashire.

Playing with the Bradshaw Cricket Club in 1941 Hartley dismissed 126 batsmen at less than ten runs per victim and his figures have still to be beaten. Another local product who played a great deal of Bolton League cricket both as professional and amateur was Frank Rushton and he left his mark by capturing all ten wickets on three occasions when playing for Eagley. Crowd figures have suffered in recent years but proof of the pulling power of Bolton League cricket came in 1949 when 16,620 spectators paid some £363 to see Heaton and Kearsley contest the Hamer Cup Final on the ground of the Bolton Cricket Club at Green Lane. One doubts whether these figures will ever be equalled or beaten for the Bolton League, in common with all other leagues, is finding it difficult to attract the spectator these days; but it is not for the want of progressive thinking, for the Bolton League has never been loth to experiment either with its rules or its conditions of play, and when the Rothman Cup was introduced the League did not hesitate to enter a competition embracing the major leagues in both the North and the Midlands. What is more its representative side held its own.

Chapter 4

The Bolton and District Association

When it was founded in 1888 the Bolton and District Cricket Association had ambitions to become the biggest and best organized cricketing league in the county. Its inaugural meeting was held in the Coffee Tavern situated in Bradshawgate, one of the main Bolton thoroughfares, and there were twenty-four clubs ready and willing to enroll in what, in those far-off days, was a real cricketing adventure. Nothing quite so ambitious as a league had been attempted before although there had been much talk and, indeed, one or two efforts to regiment some of the club cricket played in those early days. So successful was the Association that after losing several clubs during the difficult days of the first World War there were still 84 clubs affiliated to the Association and playing regularly in its various divisions and sections. One battle had been won, and the Association was still a powerful influence in Lancashire cricket but the 1930s proved even more difficult days for the officials both at club and association level.

The size of the Association was said to be unwieldy. The progressives wanted a more concentrated competition and did not like the constant threat of relegation if undergoing one difficult season. An added burden was the ever-increasing demand of builders – several clubs lost their grounds and eventually their identity. In 1930 a number of clubs broke away to form the Bolton League and the Association was faced with a long and difficult struggle to regroup and counter-attack. The task was attempted and achieved, but after the second World War only 48 teams remained in membership. These ranged from the old-established little clubs of the districts around the town, to clubs formed inside

I

the workshops and the factories and from religious bodies still with big congregations. There can hardly be a more enthusiastic or a more representative body of clubs throughout the country. Nowhere is this more in evidence than at the Association's winter prize-giving when the largest hall in Bolton is not usually big enough to hold all those who have won prizes or worked for them.

The Association, like its break-away body the Bolton League to whom there is no animosity or prejudice, has produced its fair share of good players, including two of Lancashire's most famous old-timers, Albert Ward and Walter Brearley. It has never objected to professionalism but it has never allowed it to dominate what is in essence an ideal cricketing community. Johnny Tyldesley, brother of Ernest and contemporary of George Hirst, Wilfred Rhodes and Archie MacLaren, was once a Bolton Association player and so, too, was Charlie Hallows and his uncle, Jimmy. In point of fact most of the players who went from the Bolton area to Old Trafford owed allegiance to the Association as well as to the break-away Bolton League and it would probably be foolish to attempt to define which organization had played the major role in organizing and popularizing cricket in the area.

A glance at the Association records reveals that three clubs have usually been well to the fore in the search for honours and two of them, Tonge and Farnworth, are now members of the Bolton League. But before the 'split' they had each won eight senior championships before moving on to allow the East Lancashire Paper Mills club to step up and claim pride of place. The Mills were a powerful combination in the 1930s and they took the First Division championship three years in succession, in 1932–4, and then came back for a double tilt at success again in 1936–7 – achievements without parallel in the Association area.

For sheer consistency in batting it is on record that in 1926 the Astley Bridge side must have been the most difficult to dismiss for they put together a grand total of 3,658 runs and lost only 153 wickets throughout a season in which they averaged 23.9 runs per batsman, but the best club innings is credited to Westhoughton who in 1917, when war-time conditions made cricket difficult, hit up 346 – 4 before declaring against Little Hulton. From the point of view of heavy scoring by both sides Clifton hit up 245 – 8 against the Astley and Tyldesley Colliery side who faced up to their task magnificently and replied with 251 – 8 to earn a thrilling victory with minutes to spare. This was in 1937 and old-timers who saw that match still talk of the splendid sportsmanship of all the fourteen bowlers who were employed in an unavailing attempt to master batsmen in top form.

From the other angle three clubs have been dismissed for seven runs each. Egerton were the first when, in 1898, they found the Westhoughton bowling much too good for them. In 1916 Bradshaw suffered similar humility against Social Circle and in 1943 the Astley and Tyldesley Colliery bowlers were in such great form that they ran through the ranks of Clifton whose batsmen contributed five between them but were 'boosted' somewhat by the concession of two no-balls by one over-enthusiastic bowler evidently intent on beating the lowly aggregate of 7.

Three clubs have played throughout a season without suffering defeat, Farnworth doing so along with Tonge in 1893 when, in opposition, they played two stirring drawn games, and Horwich accomplishing a similar feat in 1926. On the other hand seven teams have known what it means to fail to register even one victory in a season. The clubs were Egerton (1898), Bradshaw (1902), Darcy Lever (1909), Egerton, a second time in 1916, Clifton (1924), Whittlebrook (1926) and Chloride (1939). Individual honours bring back memories of many famous cricketers but there can seldom have been a more consistent scorer in Association cricket than Billy Greenhalgh who in his career first as an amateur and then as a professional in the Competition hit up 9,435 runs for an average of 46.02 and a highest score of 145 not out. A great little batsman was Greenhalgh and, as the Lancashire saying goes, he was in his 'pomp' in the 1947 season when, going to the wicket 21 times as the East Lancashire Paper Mills professional, he scored 1,052 runs before moving over to Radcliffe where he shared in the record opening partnership with Frank Worrell. One does not usually associate Dick Tyldesley, of Lancashire spin bowling fame, with batting form out of the ordinary but he claims the Association record for the highest individual innings when, in 1917, he hammered the Little Hulton bowlers to the tune of 175 runs on behalf of his beloved Westhoughton club where, as Dick was often heard to proclaim 'they towt us how to play t'game as it were meant to be played!'

Success with the bat that sunny afternoon did not detract from the deadliness of Tyldesley's spinners and he is one of the Association's most successful bowlers. In 1919 he had a seasonal haul of 118 wickets for Westhoughton – a club that later provided England with three more players in Bill Farrimond, Dick Pollard and Len Wilkinson. In 1928 Pat Morfee, known throughout Lancashire league cricket as the 'Kent Express', equalled Tyldesley's record figures by capturing a similar number of wickets on behalf of Heaton but in 1947 both these bowlers had to yield top place to a canny little slow left-hander by the name of Johnny Briggs, who dismissed 120 Association batsmen when playing for Edgeworth Recreation. But do not mistake this Briggs with the immortal Johnny, of Lancashire and England. They were not related, yet each bowled left-hand spinners with all the deadliness and guile associated with this form of cricketing attack. Perhaps the most telling spell of bowling in the Association records, although it is not cited as the best-ever performance, was the superb return of Bill Lewis of Heaton who in 1913 shattered Tonge by dismissing all ten batsmen for a mere five runs. Nonetheless, there are many old cricketing spectators who still point to the figures of the old Lancashire stalwart Jimmy Heap, who took all ten wickets for 31 runs for Edgeworth Recreation against Walkden Moor Methodists. Heap was then 58 years old and he hit the stumps every time!

Can anybody else lay claim to such a performance at such a ripe old cricketing age? I beg to doubt it and to add spice to the story, although I cannot vouch for its accuracy, it is still a legend in the area that Heap had the last Methodist batsman plainly lbw but cancelled all appeals with a blunt request to the umpire to 'nay, let me bowl t' bugger out'. Such an occasion was well in keeping with the cut and thrust of league cricket.

Inevitably in recent years as in the past the Bolton Association has been through troublesome times but it has survived to play a prominent part in the Lancashire cricketing scene. Not only are the batsmen, the bowlers, the fieldsmen and the wicket-keepers rewarded for meritorious performances but there are also awards for the best-kept score book and the tidiest club dressing room. Where there is such enthusiasm there is no fear for cricket!

Chapter 5

The Northern League

One of the youngest (it was founded in a break-away from the wide-stretching Ribblesdale League in 1952) leagues in Lancashire is the Northern League but already the Northern has made its mark and contributed much to the benefit of cricket in the county. It caters for a wide area beginning with Leyland in the south and taking in the coastal clubs of St Annes, Blackpool, Fleetwood and Morecambe, stretching up into the Furness area, and spreading into Cumberland where it embraces the Kendal and Netherfield clubs. The League has one of cricket's most distinguished figures, Sir Donald Bradman, as its president. Permitting professionalism but rationing it to one paid player per club the Northern League has attracted many world-famous players to Saturday and Sunday afternoon matches limited to five hours play. Prominent, both from the point of view of honours gained and in the engagement of 'big name' professionals, have been the Blackpool Cricket Club who have perhaps the most popular ground in the county outside of Old Trafford in their Stanley Park enclosure.

On this ideal league cricket venue there has been much vintage batsmanship and bowling and Rohan Kanhai, the West Indies batsman, did much to add to Blackpool's lustre and reputation in 1962 when he hit up 1,165 runs in delightful style but still did not shatter the League record of an earlier Blackpool professional – the ever-green Bill Alley who was so complete the master of bowlers in the 1953 season that he hit up 1,345 runs and had an average of 149.44 because he was so seldom dismissed. These are phenomenal figures and they enabled Blackpool to win the championship with something to spare, but even in the height of his 'golden' summer Alley could not match the splendour of Kanhai later for the brilliant West Indian hit six centuries in the course of yet another memorable season.

Primarily because of the excellence of its clubs' pitches the Northern League bowlers have always had to work harder for their wickets than in most other Lancashire leagues and so far not one bowler, fast or slow, has reached 100 wickets in a season. In 1962 Girdhari, the Indian Test player, threatened to do so when he started off in great form with Netherfield. Playing as an amateur after several seasons as the club professional Girdhari had reached the 50-wicket mark long before the half-way stage in the season but in the second half he lost touch and with bad weather also a handicap he had to be satisfied with a final haul of 70 wickets which still represents the League's best amateur return. Guy Willatt, the former Cambridge University Blue and one-time Derbyshire captain, has a niche in the League's record book when, in 1955, he hit 773 runs for the Kendal Cricket Club and set a target few amateur batsmen can hope to better although Joe Blackledge, the Chorley captain who had one unlucky season as Lancashire's leader in first-class cricket, came close to doing so when in the 1959 season he scored 761 runs and had two fewer innings than Willatt four years earlier. In addition to the League championship, fought out by first and second elevens, the Northern League has a popular Knock-out Competition for the Slater Cup and in its own sphere provides much entertaining cricket as well as setting an example of shrewd and admirable administration.

Chapter 6

The Ribblesdale League

Although it suffered much in prestige and attractiveness when the Northern League was founded in 1952, the Ribblesdale League, founded in 1893, never lost hope or faith in the future and today remains one of the oldest and most respected leagues in Lancashire doing much good work in a widely scattered area comprising a dozen clubs in a senior division and eight in a junior competition that does much to satisfy the demands of the teen-agers when they leave school and aim for the highest cricketing spheres. Earby and Settle are welcomed 'fugitives' from the Yorkshire cricketing sphere in the Ribblesdale League which in a way trespasses on the Lancashire League by including such clubs as Padiham, Blackburn Northern and Great Harwood. Before they migrated to the Northern League Blackpool set the championship pace in the League and also introduced some notable professionals including Cec Parkin and Ted McDonald in the 'boom' days of the late 1920s and early 1930s. Later came the New Zealander C. S. 'Stewie' Dempster to grace the Stanley Park and Ribblesdale scene, although perhaps the most talented of the amateur batsman was Joe Massey, a man who was once described by Lancashire's immortal Johnny Tyldesley as a 'far better batsman than many who have played for England.' Be that as it may, those who had the privilege of watching Massey at the height of his career with Blackpool and Rochdale recall a delightful batsman not only for the runs he acquired but also for the manner of their making. When such players as Sydney Barnes and Cec Parkin readily agreed with Massey's high ranking he must have been a player of exceptional ability.

The Ribblesdale League record for batsmen is held by Leslie Warburton who became Leyland's professional after World War

II and in 1949 hit up 1,356 runs for a fantastic average of 193.71. He followed this two years later by registering 1,024 runs although his average 'sank' to 78.71 in 1951! With the ball no cricketer has ever beaten the performance of George Hudson who, as Clitheroe's professional in 1949, took 124 wickets at a cost of 7.10 runs each although on two occasions, in later years Tom Edwardson (Chorley) came near with 100 victims at 7.40 and 113 at 7.77 with an astute mixture of swing and off-spin bowled on an immaculate length. Administration is by club representation and the help of a notable list of vice-presidents who form what might be termed an 'upper house' of much value from an advisory point of view and ensure that the Ribblesdale League is held in high esteem.

Chapter 7

The Lancashire and Cheshire League

Comprised of fourteen clubs from three counties, Lancashire, Cheshire and Derbyshire, the League provides high-class cricket for a scattered area around the Greater Manchester Area with Glossop representing the Derbyshire element, Stalybridge, Dukinfield, Marple and Bollington upholding Cheshire, and Cheetham, Denton, Denton St Lawrence, Norden, Longsight, Prestwich, Stand, Swinton and Unsworth, presenting the Lancashire 'threat'. Founded during the first World War, in 1915 to be precise, the Lancashire and Cheshire League has no objection to professionalism but does not enforce it and throughout the years the amateurs have usually been capable of holding their own with the paid performers although at one time Glossop, under the patronage of the influential Hill-Wood family enjoyed an opening attack of Cadman and Bestwick of Derbyshire. Marple and Norden are two recent recruits to the League, taking over from the twin district clubs of Levenshulme and East Levenshulme who were too near the centre of the city of Manchester to stand any real chance of survival in the rat race for building space of the 1950s.

Incidentally it is the proud boast of the League that some of their clubs claim roots further back than the majority of league cricket clubs. Denton, for example, can trace its beginnings back to 1824 and Stalybridge has records dated 1879 indicating the club had then been in existence several years. The first President of the League, W. H. Rhodes, was a Stalybridge man and his good example has not been lost for the club has continued to provide the League with outstanding officials as well as talented players. The present chairman, Harry Hulme, is a Stalybridge stalwart, notable for stirring batting displays on the field in his younger days and shrewd administrative qualities in committee room in his later years. A past chairman, Dick Ainsworth, of the Denton St Lawrence club, was also one of the League's most successful amateur bowlers and by and large there has been a steady flow of men from the playing field to the committee room in what is an admirable cricketing trait. There is an absence of 'records' in the League Handbook and this typifies the spirit in which the Lancashire and Cheshire League clubs play their cricket. They are essentially team efforts as distinct from outstanding personal achievements but down the years there have been many fine players associated with the League and both Dick Tyldesley and Cec Parkin held professional appointments in the League.

There were so many others perhaps not quite so renowned. I can recall Alf Cassley who learned the game at Middleton but spent almost the whole of his professional career with the Stand Cricket Club and contributed much to their success in the championship and Walker Cup spheres by canny spin bowling and hard-hitting batsmanship. Son of an old-timer in the League Alf Cassley was a real chip off the old cricketing block and there were many others besides him. Cyril Whetton, a long serving Longsight professional, was a leg-spinner whose googly was difficult to pick out and if there was ever a greater cricketing trier than Billy Dennis, of Stalybridge, I never met him. Over after over, hour after hour, Dennis, a faithful servant also to the Cheshire County Cricket Club was formidable cricketing opposition and so too was Jack Walker who played first with Stalybridge and then with Macclesfield and matched his ability to dismiss batsmen regularly and cheaply by holding hundreds of catches, scoring runs when they were needed most, and who was also adept at preparing the sort of cricketing pitch that gave both batsman and bowler a fair deal. Where are his kind today? In later years the League had few greater club men than Eric Gemmell who, like Cassley learned the game at Middleton, and who played both as a professional and an amateur with Levenshulme. Even when listed as the paid player he would often forego his wages when the weather was bad and the gate receipts negligible.

Chapter 8

The Other Leagues

Although I have singled out what may be termed the 'major' leagues for detailed reference there are others that must inevitably be classed among 'the other leagues'. I mean no disrespect in by-passing the Saddleworth and District League, an organization that borders on Lancashire, Yorkshire and Cheshire, and brings much lustre to what is essentially a village green section with all the traditions and memorable stories that surround that brand of cricket so essential to the well-being of the game. Year in and year out the Saddleworth and District League, like the Derbyshire and Cheshire League and the High Peak League, provides excellent cricket. Here, in the hills and the valleys of the three counties there is considerable local rivalry each Saturday and Sunday afternoon when the sun shines, and even when it does not for the league cricketer is a hardy creature who will turn out and enjoy his game when the 'higher-ups' of the county and international scene have decided there can be no play at all. Given a fine afternoon the league game is seldom completely immobilized and the cricket is none the worse for batsmen and bowlers having to master a mud heap of a pitch and outfield.

These three 'border' leagues and the North Lancashire League could provide enough material for yet another book spotlighting the skill, the humour and the character of league cricket and there are many more in the area doing work of a similar kind. The North Western league caters nowadays for the industrial clubs, the teams formed in the workshop, the factory, and the office, and among the entirely amateur leagues are many with a valued history and happy memories of past cricketing battles as well as with high hopes for the future – such organizations as the Fylde Cricket League, the Accrington and District League, the Chorley and

District League, the West Lancashire League, the Southport and District League, the South Lancashire League, the West Lancashire and others.

They are all an essential part of cricket in Lancashire although one must not forget the part played by two organizations which prefer to be known as spheres of club cricket but have much in common with the league game because they are both well organized and highly skilful – the Manchester and District Cricket Association and the Liverpool Competition. In recent years the Manchester Association has introduced a competitive element by playing for a club championship as well as for the love of the game. There is no obligation on any club to take part but most do because they recognize the extra incentive that comes from the award of points and the distinction of winning.

The Manchester Association was founded in 1892. The Liverpool and District Competition can also trace its history back to the 1890s and was probably in existence earlier, although it always objected to being classed as a league. It plays good class club cricket with professionalism permitted and practised on a modest scale, but it has never had an over-all committee to make rules or see that they are kept. It has relied upon local newspapers to provide a table of results and performances but has recently widened its scope by playing representative cricket against the Manchester Association and the Merseyside Competition clubs more closely linked to league principles and including several works teams. Cast not any doubts upon the club cricketer. Often he is as good if not better than his league counterpart. Lancashire may well have a preponderance of leagues, some world-famous, others almost unknown, and the county is not alone in its belief that cricket is none the worse for the spice of points, cups and championships. These are the elements that add the final touch and bring out what is best in the player, the administrator and the spectator. It is good cricket, rich in tradition, honest in assessment and down-to-earth in its approach. Who could ask for more?

Chapter 9

The Yorkshire Leagues

There are six or seven major leagues in Yorkshire and the class of cricket is no less keen, no less competitive, and certainly no less attractive than its counterpart across the Pennines, but the one big difference between them is the outlook on professionalism. In Lancashire the sky is the limit and the world the hunting ground. In Yorkshire there is moderation in what has tended to become a crippling burden; professionalism is an essential part of the game but not a dominating feature of it. The cricket is none the worse for this common sense attitude.

It is true, perhaps, to say that the Yorkshireman at all times thinks of cricket in terms of its relationship to the county side and its many championship successes and rightly or wrongly the league cricket officials of the Ridings believe it is their duty to discover and train the best young cricketers they can lay their hands upon until they are good enough to be passed on to the county club. It is a belief beyond criticism or argument. All for one and one for all is certainly the overriding principle of all cricketers in Yorkshire and the leagues do not regard themselves as anything more than a cog – admittedly an important one – in the great cricket machine that enables the county, alone in the cricket world, to proclaim that none but a Yorkshireman may play for Yorkshire.

Down the years the source of supply to the Yorkshire county side has been the leagues and the clubs. They abound in every city, every town, every village and indeed it would be difficult to travel the length and breadth of the Broad Acres and come across a community without its cricket ground. They are self-supporting and content to go their modest way. Sometimes it may be years before they unearth a player rich enough in promise to aspire to first-class standards but that is no deterrent. It is, indeed, all the more of a challenge, and when the time comes as inevitably it does, and some village cricketer travels to Leeds, to Bradford, to Sheffield or to any of the other Yorkshire County Cricket Club match venues, and makes an impression there is happiness almost beyond human understanding in the home circles. I have heard it said, by a rough hewn Yorkshireman, that if every cricket club in the county produced only one first-class player every one hundred years there would be no fear of the future. How right he was. In Yorkshire every cricketer born in the county is brought up in the belief that he should play for the county. Every club, every official and every spectator, is dedicated to the task of finding and encouraging a steady supply of talent.

Once a player makes the grade for Yorkshire the cricketing world is his for the taking and if the supply should exceed the demand, as it so often does, there are other counties, Lancashire among them, who are happy to accommodate the overflow. In times of stress, in two World Wars, for instance, the Yorkshire Leagues have opened their doors to the international players who had little or no opportunity of playing elsewhere, but they have appeared in Yorkshire on the leagues' own terms and conditions, and been happy to do so. In the first World War, Jack Hobbs, Frank Woolley, Cec Parkin and Johnny Tyldesley all took part in Bradford League cricket. In the second World War the Bradford area resounded with the names of famous players like Learie Constantine, Eddie Paynter, George Duckworth, Tom Goddard and Cyril Washbrook who travelled into Yorkshire and earned a modest pound or two when professionalism was barred, or frowned upon, nearer home. It has been said a Yorkshireman only permits the outsider to play in his midst when he will do so for nothing or next to nothing. Be that as it may there can be no denying the fact that Yorkshire cricket has thrived on this much desired 'loyalty' from the village green to the Test match scene. Would that other counties had a united cricketing front of similar strength and understanding!

The cynic will say, and often back up his assertions with facts and figures, that from the league cricket point of view some of the best Lancashire league cricketers have been Yorkshiremen and some of the Yorkshire league record holders have been Lancastrians or other 'foreigners'. This may well be true, but by and large Yorkshire cricket has been and will remain self-supporting. The leagues will see to that. In their determination to do the spade work for the county club they have the most powerful cricketing weapon in the world.

24. Rohan Kanhai, the West Indies batsman, who scored runs galore for Blackpool and Ashington.

25. Bill Alley, the Australian-born batsman who hit many runs for Colne and Blackpool before joining Somerset.

26. Gary Sobers shows the stylist touch.

27. Wes Hall demonstrates the perfect follow-through. A sight dreaded by batsman in first-class cricket as well as the Lancashire and Staffordshire leagues.

Chapter 10

The Bradford League

It is inevitable that one league more than others should stand out more clearly in the minds of the cricketing public and when one talks of league cricket in Yorkshire the yardstick with which to measure the strength and the weakness of the game in the county is the Bradford League. It was formed in 1903 and has played a prominent role ever since. It is also inevitable that the outsider should think at first of the many great players who turned out under its auspices in the two World Wars for it is as true today as ever it was that names make news. But for nearly seventy years it has been the scene of much stirring cricket and many are the batsmen, the bowlers, and the all-rounders who have learned the rudiments of cricket in the Bradford League and gone on to win world-wide repute. Not all of them have played for Yorkshire – but the vast majority did and undoubtedly will in the future. It is the names of the clubs, however, that have made history rather than the deeds of the men who play for them. Almost every Bradford League club, past and present, can trace its roots way back to the early nineteenth century.

The Bradford Cricket Club itself traces its beginnings back to 1836 and the historic Pudsey St Lawrence Club which provided Herbert Sutcliffe, Len Hutton and a number of other great players for Yorkshire, has records going back to 1845 and hint also at events even before then.

A recital of the names of the present Bradford League clubs arouses both nostalgia and the belief that cricket can never die. Taking them in alphabetical order they are: Baildon, Bankfoot, Bingley, Bowling Old Lane (what a sweet sounding name it is), Bradford, Brighouse, East Bierley, Eccleshill, Farsley, Great Horton, Hartshead Moor, Idle (yet another lovable name),

Keighley, Laisterdyke, Lidget Green, Lightcliffe, Pudsey St Lawrence (surely an aristocrat among cricket clubs), Queensbury, Saltaire, Salts, Spen Victoria, Undercliffe, Windhill, Yeadon. There you have not merely names of cricket clubs but the very essence, indeed the Yorkshire Relish, of the game at week-end level. Name me the man who would not pause to roll around his tongue some of the titles of these historic little cricket clubs whose grounds and deeds have meant so much to Yorkshire in the past. Who can doubt but that behind each and every one of them lies a story of sacrifice and hard work as well as good cricket? The Bradford League, no less than the Lancashire League, has a unique place in cricket history. Here, in town, village or hamlet, lies the true strength that has carried Yorkshire and Yorkshiremen to so many cricketing triumphs at home and abroad.

The Yorkshireman is no great respecter of age and tradition. He acknowledges them as an essential part of the past but he is never content to stand still and the Bradford League has never had cause to regret its boldness in being one of the first cricketing organizations to face up and adopt the two-division principle with the inevitable 'ups and downs' that came with it. There is no false modesty about these dour Bradford League officials. They did not hesitate to name their Divisions I and II, nor did they try to disguise the fact that to be relegated was a set-back but not a disaster. In doing so they put to shame many another cricketing league, and it is fitting they should always regard the Bradford Club and its Park Avenue ground as the centre setting for the League as a whole. It is the venue for the final of the Priestley Cup summer by summer and the one ground on which the 'special occasions' must be held. However, to the man in the street, the man outside Yorkshire, it is the sweet sounding name of the Pudsey St Lawrence club that first comes to mind and with it, of course, the fact that Herbert Sutcliffe and Len Hutton learned the game there.

Nonetheless Pudsey St Lawrence can claim no greater share of success in the Bradford League than half a dozen other clubs, either from the point of view of championships won or individual performances or when, from its foundation in 1903 to its switch to two divisions in 1937, the Bradford League set the trend with seven championship successes including a hat-trick triumph in the summers of 1927, 1928 and 1929. Since the formation of the two divisions major honours have gone to the Windhill Cricket Club but they are not too far ahead and could well be caught and passed within the space of the next few years.

From the individual point of view batting performances in particular must be divided into two categories, before and after the League once again boldly set the example by introducing time limit cricket when all around them other leagues were putting off what they considered the 'evil' day. In the days before limitation W. Payton, of Bankfoot, hit up a resounding 187 against Great Horton in 1919 and this remains the League's highest innings on record and in 1949 Arnold Hamer who played first with Yorkshire and then with Derbyshire in first-class cricket set up the League's best aggregate performance by registering 1,106 runs for Pudsey St Lawrence. Close on him comes that punishing Lancashire left-hander, Eddie Paynter, who played as much cricket in Yorkshire as he did in Lancashire at league level. In the 1942 season he averaged 138.55 for Keighley with whom he produced some sterling batsmanship bringing him also 1,040 runs in 1940 to beat the previous best by Edgar Oldroyd, the backbone of the Yorkshire batting for so many years, who in 1933 accumulated 1,034 runs for Pudsey St Lawrence.

Then came Hamer and his tally remains the target for the batsmen of the future. Bowling honours go to the one and only Sydney Barnes who, sharing his talent between Lancashire, Yorkshire and Staffordshire at league height, captured 122 wickets at the remarkably low cost of only 4.10 per victim when in deadly form for Saltaire in 1922. Barnes had, so to speak, given notice of intent in 1915 when he took five Baildon Green wickets in successive deliveries; and in later years Learie Constantine (Windhill), Emmott Robinson (Eccleshill) and Tom Goddard (Keighley) each claimed four wickets in four deliveries. Wherever Sydney Barnes played however, he commanded attention and in 1915 he produced a memorable spell of bowling to capture all ten Baildon Green wickets for 14 runs on behalf of Saltaire and in these figures included, of course, his five-in-five. Two years later Cec Parkin also captured all ten wickets at the cost of one extra run when playing for Undercliffe – and again the Baildon Green batsmen were on the receiving end. Great bowling performances indeed but by no means a record in the Bradford League where, in 1922, George Brook, playing for Keighley against Tong Moor, dismissed every batsman for a mere four runs – and that a boundary off the one loose delivery the spinner sent down! He later joined Worcestershire. And one must not forget T. A. Jacques, a fast bowler who also played quite a bit of league cricket in Lancashire, but seldom shattered the batsman as he did in the Bradford League in 1933 when he claimed all ten wickets for 25 runs and hit the stumps each time.

Glancing through the Bradford League handbook, one comes across famous names galore – and not all of them were Yorkshire cricketers. Winston Place and Cyril Washbrook, so often paired together at the start of a Lancashire innings, enjoyed themselves, and at times knew failure as well as success, in the League sphere as did Wally Keeton of Nottinghamshire and George Pope of Derbyshire. But one looks, perhaps not in vain, but certainly without much success for the names of Herbert Sutcliffe and Len Hutton. They were Bradford League players, of course, but they do not exactly stand out as scorers of runs. They must have added tone to the scene but it is a striking tribute to the Bradford League and they had to fight, and fight hard, for recognition.

Indeed, one of the reasons for the continued success and popularity of the Bradford League lies in it's intense 'local' atmosphere, its stirring clashes between the local boys and the professionals who are not, of course, importations in the sense that they come from abroad or indeed from other counties but simply that they are not born and bred in the vicinity of the club for whom they play. It would be correct, give or take a mile or two in any direction, to assume that the area covered by the Bradford League consists of some twenty-five square miles and that any player who travels more than ten miles for his weekly cricket is regarded as a nomad. In war time it was different, with so many big-name players available that the Bradford League wisely offered them opportunity to keep both in practice and in the limelight. The cost may have seemed heavy from the casual observer's point of view but by the standards of the Lancashire and Central Lancashire Leagues there has never been a lot of money paid out for professional assistance. The strength of the League lies in a high amateur standard and there can be no greater tribute to this than the fact Yorkshire County Cricket Club never failed to take what opportunities arose to 'allocate' their colts to clubs in the Bradford League.

In their wisdom the county officials knew that a batsman or a bowler, willing and anxious to improve his standards, could not do better than engage in weekly Bradford League battles. He would come up against formidable opposition. A batsman would find himself faced with a variety of bowling to test his reactions and his reflexes; a bowler would find opposing batsman capable not only of playing shots but also of taking heavy toll of loose deliveries. In the field woe betide an erring fieldsman or a slow-moving one. From the tactical point of view there was no let-up. Captaincy may have been somewhat rough-tongued, tinged with bluff words and savoured with discipline, and no matter what one's background the essential requirement of the Bradford League was, and still is, to provide the essential qualities of fighting cricket. There is no room for the cricketing innocent. A Bradford League match is in itself a battle: a sporting one but, nonetheless, a battle.

I know several players of international repute who regarded the League as the most testing of all cricketing spheres. George Duckworth frequently expressed the opinion that the strength of Yorkshire cricket lay in the manner in which its players were taught to play it – in the Bradford League in particular. He told stories of lbw appeals from square leg, run out demands from the boundary edge, and even requests to the umpires to watch out for bowlers overstepping the crease and batsmen from stealing inches when backing up. And Duckworth really loved this sort of cricketing warfare. It kept a man on his toes. There was more to cricket in the Bradford League than scoring runs, taking wickets and holding catches. One had to be quick of tongue as well as agile of movement. It was often necessary to administer rough justice and one of Duckworth's favourite stories concerned a local player renowned for his big hitting and coming to the wicket when ten runs were wanted for victory in the last over. Another old-timer had the ball and the captain of the fielding side, anxious to win but ever conscious of losing, counselled caution. 'Bowl 'em down t'leg side, George,' was the gist of his advice. 'Nay, skipper, ahm going to bowl at bloddy stumps. If he hits 'em it'll be just too bad. But if ah hits him that's all in't game,' was the retort. And Duckworth, the batsman at the non-striking end, never failed to chuckle when he told how the last man in clobbered two fours, missed two more, and was bowled middle stump off the fifth delivery. Honour was satisfied, all round. It was cricket typical of the Bradford League.

And there was reward for the brave. Collections for meritorious performances with bat and ball have always been part and parcel of the League scene and Learie Constantine, as popular a cricketer as any foreigner could be amongst Yorkshiremen, swears to the truth of the story of a left-hander who played regularly for Yorkshire for a time but was far happier in the leagues, and who week after week boosted his salary as a club professional with neatly timed batting and bowling returns. There was, however, one occasion when he cut it rather fine. Only four runs were needed to win the match and the much travelled left-hander had lost the bowling. Worse than that the crowd was preparing to leave and all was nearly lost – from the financial point of view. But the old pro had the answer. He instructed his amateur colleague to take a single. 'Ahm 47 and need three more for a collection. Thee get t'single and ah'll hit next ball for four. Then ahm going to dash to gate and tak my own collection – so drop thi bat and give me a lift.' The plan worked. The pro got his 50 and his collection, his side won the match and everybody was happy. That was cricket in the Bradford League!

Chapter 11

The Huddersfield and District League

Long before the Bradford League was formed there was league cricket in the Huddersfield area of Yorkshire and in 1891 onwards the Huddersfield and District League was formed. Did it not provide those two cricketing 'twins', George Hirst and Wilfred Rhodes, with the opportunity to learn and practise before moving into the world of bigger cricket? Did it not also allow them to go back and wind up their careers in the hills and valleys that provide the clubs with colourful names like Almondbury, Broad Oak, Hall Bower, Holmfirth, Huddersfield, Kirkburton, Lascelles Hall, Lockwood, Meltham, Rastrick, Thongsbridge, Armitage Bridge, Bradley Mills, Dalton, Elland, Golcar, Honley, Linthwaite, Marsden, Paddock, Primrose Hill, Shepley and Slaithwaite? Here professionalism is permitted but it has always been practised on a modest scale. Modest, that is, from the financial point of view.

Years ago – and one is happy to think it was in the days when the men who ruled the League journeyed from the nearby villages and hamlets in horse-drawn vehicles – labourers in the woollen mills rubbed shoulders with the mill managers as they sat round the committee table to define the meaning of the cricket 'amateur'. It was necessary, one believes, because all the League clubs did not see eye to eye on what constituted payment, be it in coppers or in gold sovereigns. To their revelasting credit it was resolved then, and still applies today, that an amateur in the Huddersfield League is a player who 'receives no cash payment or any other reward for playing cricket or for other services to his club either from his club or on behalf of his club. Or from, or on behalf, of any other person or body connected with his club.' Long-winded?

Maybe, but certainly all-embracing and observed, one might add, throughout the League from that day until this.

The League, like most others, is governed by club representatives and always the emphasis has been on the club and not the individual. There is no mention in the League Handbook of the best batting or bowling performances by either amateur or professional, yet in the area around Huddersfield the cricketing public have their record breakers and their giants in all departments of the game. It is recorded that in the first year of its existence, when the League was not, as now, divided into sections, two clubs, Armitage and Slaithwaite tied for the championship. Perhaps it has never been so close a race for honours since but there can be no denying that before the split into two divisions in 1932 the Huddersfield Club, as befits the centrepiece of the League, won the senior championship on eleven occasions and took the Sykes Cup, the League's Knock-out Trophy, six times. Not far behind comes the old-established Elland club which boasts that way back in 1878 they were one of the few club sides honoured with a fixture against the first Australian touring team to visit England. Three years earlier W. G. Grace played on the Huddersfield ground in a North v. South battle that somehow or other appears to have missed the attention of cricket's historians.

The passage of time has, alas, seen the demise of several of the League's founder clubs but Kirkheaton, the birthplace of Rhodes and Hirst will never lose its reputation or its place in Yorkshire cricketing history. It is on record that in 1904 Hirst with his swing and pace, and Rhodes, with his variation of spin and flight, put to rout the nearby Slaithwaite batsmen who were dismissed for nine runs with Hirst taking 5 – 2 and Rhodes 4 – 3 with the odd man run out. It is said of both of them that they were costly acquisitions to the local cricketing scene once they had made their name; but Rhodes has remembered on more than one occasion the most he ever got for playing for Kirkheaton was a golden sovereign and Hirst is believed to have seldom achieved such rewards.

Chapter 12

Leeds and District League

It is at Headingley that the county club plays and from the palatial new offices there (at square leg to the batsman facing the bowling from the football end) that the secretary, John Nash, supervises the whole cricketing structure of the county. Naturally Leeds has its own league cricket and in Leeds and District League there is an organization that embodies both district clubs and works teams in two divisions, and in addition to championships which also puts up for knock-out competition the Hepworth and the Wood Cups. Among the clubs that contribute are: Carlton, Gildersom e, Hunslet Nelson, Lofthouse, Pudsey Britannia, Whitkirk, Woodhouse, Yorkshire Copper Works, Clayton Sports, Colton, East Leeds, Garforth, Holbeck, Highbury Works, Kirkstall Education, Leeds City Police, L.I.C.S., Whitehall Printeries and Rothwell. It is a miscellaneous cricketing area bound by industry and fighting ever-increasing battles for land.

Nonetheless the League fights on and it is recorded, with some degree of justification that the Holbeck club appears to take the lion's share of senior championship honours and Hepworth Cup successes but it is by no means a case of one club monopolizing the other.

In the past the League has provided many fine players as professionals for other leagues – especially in Lancashire – and it appears content to be the training ground for youngsters. Certainly there are few famous names in the record book but occasionally one comes across a name to be remembered. Billy Newton was one who aroused nostalgic memories for me. What a bonny fighter was this craggy Yorkshire all-rounder. A fast bowler who never knew the meaning of the word 'surrender' or acknowledged defeat until the last run had been scored or the last wicket taken.

Billy was a force to be reckoned with in Central Lancashire League cricket in the 1930s and he was still creating problems for both batsmen and bowlers for Holbeck in the 1950s. Horace Fisher was another and he, like Newton, spent the twilight of a great career in the Leeds and District League.

Without such leagues Yorkshire cricket in particular, and English cricket in general, would be much the poorer. Not so long ago Emmott Robinson and I were discussing the standing of the various leagues in Lancashire and Yorkshire and Emmott would not accept the common belief that the Lancashire League stands supreme. He did not exactly say so but I imagine he was thinking in terms of highly-paid professionalism when he simply ended the debate with 'all that glitters is not gold!' He had as high an opinion of the Leeds and District League and others of the same calibre as he had of the more fashionable and certainly more publicised leagues. Trust Emmott to sort out the cricketing wheat from the chaff.

Chapter 13

The Yorkshire League

Yorkshire, like Lancashire with the Manchester and District Association and the Liverpool Competition, has an organization that cannot completely fit into the league cricket scene. The Yorkshire Council is the backbone of purely amateur cricket but in its midst it has a league section – the Yorkshire League. Alongside is the Central Yorkshire League and both were formed without separation from the Council clubs who desired and demanded a more competitive form of cricket at week-ends. In 1968 Leeds won the Yorkshire League championship and in the Central Yorkshire League Wakefield, astutely led by Vic Wilson, the first professional to be officially appointed captain of the Yorkshire County Cricket Club, took the title after a season of much enjoyment and much fine cricket. Although the practice is on the wane now Yorkshire used to allocate the best of their up-and-coming young cricketers to clubs in the Council and the League which embodies such clubs as Barnsley, Castleford, Doncaster Town, Halifax, Harrogate, Hull, Leeds, Rotherham Town, Scarborough, Sheffield Collegiate, Sheffield United and York: the senior citizens of the county as it were. The League's matches are played under the time-limit system and an unusually high award of five points goes to the winner of an outright victory – one won, as it were, by shrewd captaincy and clever cricket in a race against the clock and the elements. It is a system that appears to work well although, inevitably, the scheme has its critics and there was in recent years a marked falling off in spectator appeal. Happily the trend appears to be over and, although crowds are still far from big or satisfactory, this is an aspect that does not unduly worry either League or club officials. After all it is the game that counts.

Hull appeared to be the early pace setters in the League and at one time they drew well ahead of their rivals with nine championships to their name including triple successes in 1936–8 and again in 1947–9 but today there is a much more noticeable 'levelness' about the competition and the battle for honours is all the keener for the spreading of ability and performance. Records, with bat and ball, are not regarded as of great importance but it is worth noting that in 1959 Billy Sutcliffe, son of Herbert and a former Yorkshire player and captain in his own right, hit up a total of 1,005 runs for Leeds and earned himself an average of some 67 runs an innings by consistent and often attractive stroke play which so frequently eluded him when playing and leading Yorkshire. Here, is a very fine cricketer, often too harshly judged by comparison with a famous father.

Ted Lester, another Yorkshire batsman of repute, earns a place among the League's outstanding run scorers with an innings of 180 for Scarborough against Hull in 1960 but the best return of any bowler in a league where wickets tend to favour the batsmen is a modest haul of 76 wickets by Peter Ellis, of Rotherham Town, in 1952. There can seldom have been anything better to watch than the partnership of 261 between T. Hobson and S. Robinson playing for York against Doncaster in 1938 but no team has yet bettered the 290 – 2 that Scarborough recorded against Halifax in 1952, although there must have been considerable satisfaction amongst the Harrogate and Scarborough players when they recorded 523 runs between them one glorious summer afternoon. Harrogate must have surely imagined themselves safe from defeat when declaring at 261 – 6 but Scarborough won and the match ended with their total standing at 262 – 6 in what must have been a titanic cricketing struggle for the bowlers.

There are many other leagues in Yorkshire doing the ideal sort of job league cricket inspires. The Airedale and Wharfedale League was one of the first to approach a Lancashire league for a representative match; and it was a happy thought that saw the inauguration at junior level of matches between the Yorkshire organization and the Central Lancashire League. The Airedale and Wharfedale has fellow leagues in abundance, with the Bradford Central

League and the Wakefield and District Union foremost among them. Each and every one has a part to play in the overall pattern of Yorkshire and English cricket.

Chapter 14

The Midland Leagues

League cricket in the Midlands concerns four counties, Warwickshire, Worcestershire, Derbyshire and Staffordshire, and it would be a risky business attempting to nominate the 'best' league in an area widely scattered and vastly different in environment. Who, for example, could imagine a greater transition than from the delightful agricultural areas of Worcestershire to the grimy industrial towns of the 'Black Country'? Yet cricket, especially league cricket, thrives in the drab surroundings equally as well as it does in the more picturesque.

Primarily because its roots go farthest back I am according pride of place in the Midlands to the Birmingham and District League, founded officially in 1888, but operating many years before that time as the Birmingham Cricket Association, and embodying all the leading clubs in Warwickshire and Worcestershire, with an occasional excursion into Staffordshire. One of the staunchest supporters of the Birmingham League is the enthusiastic secretary of the Warwickshire County Cricket Club, Mr Leslie Deakins, who seldom misses an opportunity to tell me he considers it to be the strongest league in the country – and bases his belief on a close and long connection with both players and officials.

He has also provided me with positive proof of the determination and enthusiasm with which the League is controlled by allowing me to look at correspondence and records plainly indicating an admirable and long-established cricketing community that at present comprises ten powerful clubs: Aston Unity, Kidderminster, Mitchell and Butlers, Moseley, Old Hill, Smethwick, Stourbridge, Walsall, and West Bromwich Dartmouth. Amongst the originators of the League were also Mitchell

Salters, Handsworth Wood and the Warwickshire Club and Ground – names to suggest its sponsors represented organizations of high standard and playing repute. The League was formed on the basis of the Football League, a fact established in an excellent little 'history' of the competition written by H. Grosvenor Hill on the completion of the first ten years of its being. The Birmingham League has come a long way since then. It has grown in stature and in influence with each passing year.

The League has always sanctioned professionalism. Yet it has never allowed it to obliterate or even challenge the preponderance or the performances of its high-class amateur players. And high-class they undoubtedly were and still are. Mr Deakins rightly pays tribute to the League for its constant provision and encouragement of youngsters who must inevitably and eventually form the backbone of the Warwickshire county side despite a present trend to strengthen a lean spell by special registrations of leading West Indies batsmen and bowlers. One of the objects when the League was formed was to promote the best interest of local cricket consistent with loyalty to county cricket and nobly has this ideal been accomplished.

Warwickshire and Worcestershire have frequently been happy to 'qualify' players through the medium of the League. Tom Pritchard, the New Zealand fast bowler, spent several years in the Birmingham League before he could play for Warwickshire, and Worcestershire have in recent times been happy to allow Basil D'Oliveira to qualify with Kidderminster, while Tom Graveney spent a season with Dudley when he was refused permission to move from Gloucestershire to Worcestershire without a year's qualification. Prior to that Dick Howorth, a Bacup left-hander turned away from Old Trafford, went into the Birmingham League as an essential part of his grooming for a splendid playing career with Worcestershire. In fact it is fair comment to suggest the Birmingham and District League has done more for Warwickshire and Worcestershire than has the Lancashire League for Lancashire. Certainly the League enjoyed the pleasure of the company of a great many star players migrating to county cricket from other spheres. Prominent among them, before World War II, were George Headley, the stylish West Indies batsman, the New Zealander Bill Merritt and George Brook, the Yorkshire spinner who moved on from Littleborough to Dudley en route for Worcestershire. Brook, like several other league cricketers I could name, was never flattered by figures but was always a very good player.

There was a time, in the early 1950s, when unwanted Lancashire players were attracted to the Birmingham League. Dick Pollard certainly played for one team and Bill Roberts for another and Lancashire's loss was the Midlands' gain. Northamptonshire have also been grateful to the Birmingham League for helping Jock Livingston and Albert Nutter to keep in practice whilst awaiting qualification for first-class cricket, but primarily the League's main function was to provide the means of producing and training their own players for their own counties. Warwickshire owed much to Eric Hollies and Tom Dollery in the immediate post-war years and Worcestershire, likewise, enjoyed as well as employed Reg Perks, Peter Jackson and Roly Jenkins all of whom learned their cricket in the League. I have heard Hollies proclaim not once but several times there was no harder training ground for the young player than the Birmingham League and Dollery, one of the best professional captains in first-class cricket, was another who always paid tribute to the demands of the League on the up and coming youngster.

Likewise I have heard other old players with a vast experience in various counties and other leagues, indicate that they considered the standard of play in the Birmingham League of a higher standard than elsewhere. One was Jack Holroyd who seldom failed to get seventy or eighty wickets a season in the Lancashire and Central Lancashire leagues but when he tried a spell with Kidderminster in the Birmingham League he considered himself a much better bowler in struggling to reach the 50-wicket mark. Roy Tattersall, so summarily dismissed by Lancashire, was another who found success elusive in the Midlands where pitches usually are of better quality and the opposition strong if figures are to be allied to facts and the truth be told. Warwickshire had few harder workers than Charlie Grove, a seam bowler of great persistence

28. Basil D'Oliveira pictured during his Central Lancashire League days at Middleton.

29. A familiar face in unfamiliar surroundings. Trevor Bailey, former Essex and England all-rounder, is dismissed when playing for the International Cavaliers against a Lancashire League XI in 1968.

30. A scene from the Birmingham League—Mosley in opposition to Kidderminster on their ground at Solihull.

and mighty endeavour. He used to toil on and on. Seldom did he complain but always he insisted county cricket was no harder than Birmingham League cricket although he never forgot to add the rider 'except that it lasts longer!' Grove learned to play cricket the hard way in the Midlands and he typified all that is best in the game. He was, in simple parlance, a great trier – and the Birmingham League bred them by the dozen. It is not an organization that pays much regard to figures or records and none are to hand. This must not be taken as a drawback. I prefer to look upon it as the seal of greatness, as a plain indication that it is not the individual or even the club that matters most. Of top importance is the playing of the game.

Chapter 15

The North Staffordshire and District League

Ever since 1889 the North Staffordshire and District League has been provided many fine players and a multitude of thrilling matches around the Stoke-on-Trent area. Closely linked with the Staffordshire County Cricket Club, the League caters for the 'Five Towns' area made so popular by Arnold Bennett's novels but it also extends into parts of Cheshire and to the borders of Derbyshire where rivalry and local partisanship is every bit as keen as in the Lancashire and the Yorkshire leagues. Competition is divided into two sections. So determined were the clubs that, in the winter of 1962–3 when they were so much at variance over the future of the League, there came a regrettable split, or so it appeared at the time, resulting in the migration of all the Section A clubs to form a new league, the North Staffordshire and South Cheshire League. But the older organisation recruited new members and carried on with great success even if they lost some public support to the new body which at once attracted some world famous professionals.

Few people nowadays give the League its full title and it is sufficient to refer to the Staffordshire League and be understood. Professionalism was always permitted but until recent years it was on a modest scale with the League content to act as a nursery for the Staffordshire County Cricket Club which has always been held in high esteem in Minor County circles. Year in and year out the League was not only the training ground for the county side but also its main provider of playing venues with conditions varying from highly industrialized areas to the charming rural grounds like Ashcombe Park set amid rolling pastureland and yet not too far off the beaten track to attract the crowds and retain the infectious and often partisan brand of spectatorship which is so very much part and parcel of league cricket.

One of the happiest features of the League until its split was the number of families regularly producing fine players and hard workers. Prominent among them have been the Ikin family, father, son and now grandson, all figuring notably with the Bignall End club in particular and the Staffordshire League in general. Closely on their heels, and, indeed, often playing side by side, came the Crump family, father Stanley and son Brian. Stanley Crump was a fine all-round cricketer who like two or three other Staffordshire stalwarts, notably Syd Barnes, Aaron Lockett and Joe Boon, did not hesitate to move over and add lustre to the Lancashire leagues from time to time without ever losing or denying themselves the privilege of playing for Staffordshire and eventually returning home to play, to coach, and generally provide experienced advice on and off the field.

John Ikin, of course, joined Lancashire before World War II and eventually played for England at home and abroad. His father before him had been the mainstay of the Bignall End club for years and a Minor County player rated good enough to hold his own in the best company. Now it is Michael, the third Ikin generation to keep the Staffordshire flag flying and although John Ikin's appearances are getting fewer and fewer not many men have worked harder for Staffordshire cricket than this England and Lancashire left-hander who was one of the bonniest fighters I have seen at the crease or in the field. It was the same with the Crumps. Father Stanley was always a difficult man to face with his off-spinners and cutters that accounted for many batsmen in the best of league and Minor County cricketing spheres and now his son Brian is a mainstay of the Northamptonshire side. David Steele was of the same cricketing background. His father was a sound all-rounder and it is one of the most pleasing features of Staffordshire cricket to see the same names repeatedly in the news. From grandfather to father and from father to son there is usually a link in Staffordshire cricket. And one must not forget Ken Higgs, the recently retired Lancashire and England bowler, was also a product of the Staffordshire League and there has never been a lack of promising players ready and anxious to step up when the better ones move on. It is a happy thought that the pattern continues.

In Staffordshire, as in Lancashire, the League records are dotted with famous names. It would be impossible not to start with the deeds of Sydney Barnes who often professed he enjoyed his cricket in Staffordshire to a greater degree than he did elsewhere. The great man was always a bowler to be feared, yet Barnes could never quite match the deadliness of the West Indies spinner Sonny Ramadhin, who spent three seasons with Ashcombe Park and, in his first summer with this picturesque little club in 1958, captured 125 wickets at a cost of only 5.4 runs per wicket to be followed a year later with a haul of 101 victims at just over six runs each and completed by a third-year tally of 93 victims, again at a cost of only 6.6 runs each. Ramadhin certainly cast a magical spell over the Staffordshire and District League batsmen but he was not the only one. Dick Tyldesley, the Lancashire spinner, had a happy time with Nantwich in the 1932 season when he was responsible for the dismissal of 106 batsmen at just over seven runs each, but Ramadhin and Tyldesley were simply players who graced the Staffordshire scene and then moved on.

The real strength of the League's cricket is best illustrated by the old-timers who remained loyal year after year and were well content to play league and minor county cricket with no thought of reward other than local fame and popularity. Such a man was E. H. Steventon, an amateur cricketer who was the mainstay of the Nantwich side for some twenty years and captured 1,554 wickets to prove it. Has there ever, in any league cricket sphere, been a man who contributed quite so much in terms of playing, of leadership and then of administrative duties, for Steventon was captain of his club and his county for many years and, when finally he stepped down from regular cricket, he turned to committee work and was honoured with the league presidency in 1956–8.

It is said of Steventon that his best season was in 1935 when he dismissed 106 batsmen for little more than eight runs each and there was no finer example of the loyal league cricketer than this Nantwich stalwart who year after year provided problems for the batsmen, got his share of runs when they were wanted most, fielded with great effect near or far from the wicket, and then, when it was no longer possible for him to play, proved equally valuable at the committee table as he had been at the crease. His example inspired others to achieve repute as local cricketers who could hold their own and often outshine the big-name professionals. F. Taylor, who divided his cricketing loyalties between Burslem and Stone, was at his best at the same time as Steventon and in his three vintage years of 1937–9 Taylor captured 286 wickets at an average cost of six runs each. His seasonal haul in 1937 was 89 victims at 7.3, followed a year later by the dismissal of 100 batsmen at 5.9 and, in 1939, some 97 victims came Taylor's way at a cost of 6.4 runs each – figures that denote exceptional ability. Ten years later, with World War II intervening, Taylor was still a deadly bowler for in 1948, switching his allegiance to the Stone club, he captured 98 wickets for a mere six runs each.

But the best was still to come! By no means a young man Taylor at 51 bowled better than ever in 1949 to set up a League record of 131 wickets at 6.6 each and two years later, still dropping the ball on the length that matters, Taylor returned to Burslem and dismissed 105 batsmen at the still ridiculously low cost of seven runs each. He was still going strong in 1953 when he had figures of 86 wickets at 7.2 each and, on his own admission, all he ever did was 'move the ball a little either way in the air and off the pitch.' Barnes and Lockett may well have been the most feared Staffordshire bowling combination but Steventon and Taylor were never far behind.

Turning to the batsmen who have delighted the Staffordshire and District League followers none contributed more in terms of style and power than Frank Worrell who joined Longton for three vintage seasons and hit 2,727 runs and set the trend for the engagement of other world-famous players like Trevor Goddard, the South African all-rounder who, in 1962, set up a new batting record with 1,128 runs and an average of 94 for the Great Chell club. The highest individual record is held by a 'local', A. K. Walker of Norton, who hit a superb 171 in 1955 to beat the 169 credited to Porthill Park's A. A. Bickerton in 1933 when, it is often said, the League was at its strongest. Be that as it may. Such assertions are usually the starting points of great arguments and there is no real solution for one generation will never readily accept the views of another. Let it suffice for each to nurse and remember its own highlights and simply record that down the years the Staffordshire and District League has provided cricket at its best, and pay tribute not only to the great batsmen and bowlers who have played their part but also to men of influence who have taken high office, such as past presidents like the Earl of Lichfield and the Duke of Sutherland. They lend distinction to a League which, in turn, pays tribute to the minor leagues like the Kidsgrove and District Junior League and the Leek and Stone District leagues who readily provide the raw material and the youngsters of promise. Great names and fine deeds assure the League of an important place in the official history of league cricket which has yet to be written.

Chapter 16

The North Staffordshire and South Cheshire League

It was in the winter of 1962–3 that the North Staffordshire and South Cheshire League came into being as a 'break-away' body from the Staffordshire and District League. At the time there was some discontent and even ill-feeling at the rift brought about by what was termed 'a reluctance on the part of the old-established league to move with the times', but whatever the pros and cons of the argument a new and powerful league came into being and now Staffordshire cricket is all the stronger for an 'extra' competition. The founder clubs were Bignall End, Crewe LMR, Great Chell, Knypersley, Leek, Longton, Nantwich, Newcastle and Hartshill, Norton, Porthill Park, Sneyd and Stone and that is the way the league remains today. Already it has shown itself enterprising and ambitious. Its clubs have vied with the Lancashire and Central Lancashire leagues in tempting the world-famous professionals, foremost among them being Gary Sobers, Cec Pepper and Wes Hall and if, as yet, 'record' batting and bowling feats are of little consequence to a league in its infancy it is pleasing to record the big name professionals are not having things all their own way.

In its very first year the man at the top of the batting averages was John Ikin (Bignall End) and for all-round cricket of prime importance I commend the work of the old Surrey player Dennis Cox who took 67 wickets and hit 594 runs to help Crewe LMR to the championship of the First Division. These figures may look modest in comparison with those so regularly produced in the older-established spheres but opportunity is limited when a league with only twelve clubs provides a mere 22 matches and no cup competition to provide extra competitive interest. Cox's figures stand up well when placed alongside those of Sobers who in 1964 captured 97 wickets and hit 549 runs for Norton and also achieved another 'distinction' that did not show in the scorebook and did not come to light until a mid-winter inquest when, at a club dinner, a colleague somewhat casually disclosed that one of Sober's caught and bowled victims was actually caught in front of the sight screen from a mighty hit safely chased and held by him after a shouted 'leave it to me' to the rest of the team. One wonders if Learie Constantine, generally acknowledged the best fieldsman of his time, ever achieved a similar dismissal?

So far no bowler in the League has yet topped the 100 wicket mark but eventually one will and maybe there will come a batsman capable of hitting 1,000 runs or more. One hopes it will be a Staffordshire-born cricketer who achieves the distinction for the spectator likes nothing better than to see the local boy outshine the world-famous professional. It remains one of league cricket's greatest incentives that an amateur should outplay a professional and sooner or later the North Staffordshire and South Cheshire League is bound to produce a man who can rise to the occasion. It will, inevitably, be wellnigh impossible to forget the majesty of Sobers or the deadliness of Pepper who, in his first year with Norton, dismissed 87 batsmen by his varied and often vicious spinners, but some future chronicler of the League's affairs will surely be able to point with pride to the name of a local boy who rubbed shoulders with the great and eventually came out best. Not only the writer but the League's followers as a body will rejoice and proclaim the great moment and savour it for ever. It is what league cricket is all about and I never see the name or recall the importance of the time when the Knypersley Cricket Club took, on my recommendation, a mere stripling of a fast bowler from the Middleton club in the Central Lancashire League, and gave him his first professional opportunity.

His name was Frank Tyson. To their credit this little Staffordshire club, one of the founder members of the North Staffordshire and South Cheshire League, played their part in the production of a great fast bowler. Sooner or later Knypersley, or some other league club, will do it again and another Tyson will be enabled and encouraged to take on the best in the world because he was part and parcel of the league cricket scene. It is to this end that the men who play and those who administrate in league affairs strive. They seek no high reward but keep the cricketing flag flying and occasionally, as did the men who fought for progress and founded the North Staffordshire and South Cheshire League, branch out or break away from the fold to try something new and something bold. In doing so they risk criticism, even abuse, but if there was no spirit of adventure, no desire to seek new pastures, and no attempt to live dangerously there would be no point in carrying on. League cricket, like life itself, calls repeatedly for new outlets and new challenges. They must be faced – as they were in Staffordshire just a few years ago!

Chapter 17

The Bassetlaw and District League

One of the secrets of league cricket is its parochialism. It is the intimate atmosphere of local rivalry that has made the Lancashire League great and the closer the embrace the keener the competition. Yet there are leagues, in the north and in the midlands, that thrive on wider horizons. Such a one is the Bassetlaw and District League catering for clubs in Derbyshire, Staffordshire, Nottinghamshire and Yorkshire, areas of great industrial intensity and pleasant agricultural prosperity. Scattered is a term that could, perhaps, be allied to a League proudly boasting four divisions and some 48 clubs. In many respects the League is the biggest in the country. It was founded in 1904 and is governed by a Management Committee consisting of ten representatives from the 'A' Division and three from 'B' Division. Broadly speaking the League is based on Chesterfield and it is from the town of the Crooked Spire that the League spans out to take in works organizations, colliery teams and town and village sides reaching out to Doncaster, to Mansfield, to Worksop and embodying several Sheffield area clubs. Championship honours have been widely spread with Worksop prominent in the early days but rather fading out of the picture in more recent years.

In the League Handbook there is no mention of the many outstanding batting and bowling feats that must have been returned over the years but I gather this is an aspect of the League's history that is being looked into by officials at the moment. Certainly when the League first branched out into representative cricket on the introduction of the Rothman Cup Competition it more than held its own with the more publicised Lancashire and Yorkshire leagues.

Besides the Bassetlaw and District League there are others who are all contributing to the good of cricket in the Midlands, and one recalls with appreciation, the hard work that goes into the continual struggle against rising costs and ever-encroaching possession of land for building purposes, such organizations as the West Bromwich and District League, the Birmingham Public Parks Association, the Coventry Works Sports Association, the Kidderminster and District League and the Smethwick and District League. In the words of Warwickshire County Cricket Club's popular secretary, Leslie Deakins, they surely 'do much good in the great world of cricket'.

Also in the Midlands is the Lincolnshire County League which does a splendid job for week-end cricketers and spectators. The strength of this widely scattered league can be judged from the fact its representative side won the Rothman Cup in 1967 and 1968 beating off the challenge of the major Lancashire and Yorkshire leagues with something to spare. If there is an absence of big cricketing names among the clubs that does not mean the cricket lacks sparkle; and the League's two Rothman Cup victories are pointers to a bright future.

Chapter 18

The North-East Leagues

In the areas of Northumberland and Durham surrounding the three great rivers, the Tees, the Tyne and the Wear, there is also much good cricket in several major leagues and a host of smaller ones. It is not only Minor County but first-class cricket that has benefited, and one has only to mention two names, Colin Milburn and Jim McConnon, to realize how the North-East has provided top-class players for England and for various counties. Far and wide the cricketers of the North-East travel to gain recognition and in recent years Lancashire has brought Gerry Knox and David Bailey down to Old Trafford and given them the opportunity of branching out into the best cricketing company. The North Yorkshire and South Durham League is usually regarded as one of the major leagues in this part of the country but you will never get officials to press the claim. They are content to be considered part and parcel of the league cricket scene in the area. Its formation goes back to 1893 and at present the League comprises some 24 clubs playing in two divisions.

In addition to its championships, the hall-mark of consistent endeavour throughout the whole of the season, the League also provides an outlet for those who like their sport based on the knock-out principle with the Kerridge Cup and the Haith Cup. The season, which spreads from early April to mid-September, never lacks for keenness or ability. If three clubs, Darlington, West Hartlepool and Middlesbrough appear to have been the most consistent of sides there is plenty of evidence that their successes have had to be earned the hard way, for few run-away victories are recorded. The League originally began life as the North Yorkshire League after an inaugural meeting at Thirsk in 1893 with six clubs sharing 'foundation' honours. They were: Constable Burton, Ironopolis (surely a unique cricketing title),

Middlesbrough, Northallerton, Redcar and Thirsk. There have been some sticky moments both on the field and off, and it is recorded that on one occasion the League Management Committee had to deal drastically with an umpire who reported for duty the worse for drink and demanded an increase of one shilling in his wages before he took the field. Alas the action taken is not revealed but one doubts whether in any cricketing sphere an intoxicated umpire would be tolerated.

Professionalism has played a modest part in the league but there are many names of repute figuring in the league's book of performances with Cec Parkin, a man of many cricketing parts, learning the game with Norton and E. W. Clark, better known as 'Nobby', of Northamptonshire fame, also being brought up in the area. Among others there are four Somerset players of great ability in Maurice Tremlett (Darlington RA), Harold Stephenson (Stockton and Synthonia), Maurice Walford (Norton) and Horace Hazell (Synthonia). Worcestershire benefited greatly between the wars by the signing of Victor Fox (Middlesborough) and George Brook (Stockton) and Warwickshire recruits from the North-Eastern area were Dick Spooner (Norton) and Alan Townsend (Thornaby) – all cricketers who went south as professionals and did much for their adopted counties.

There have also been several top-class amateurs trained and encouraged in the League, foremost among them being the Towsend brothers, C. L. and D. C. H. who left Norton to add lustre to Gloucestershire cricket. C. L. Townsend must have been one of the most attractive and consistent batsmen in the North Yorkshire and South Durham League for he contributed 9,390 runs during an illustrious career. His brother, who also played for Winchester and Oxford University added further distinction to the scene by astute captaincy of the Durham team in Minor County cricket. The Doggart family were another North-East cricketing contingent. A. G. contributed much sparkle on behalf of the Bishop Aukland club and J. H. and N. A. were stalwart players for Darlington. All in all the North Yorkshire and South Durham League holds a prominent place in the sporting life of the North-Eastern area.

Founded in 1902 the Durham Senior League has a happy history. It has no objection to professionalism but does not allow it to run riot and whilst its rules and regulations are fewer than most leagues of its kind they are guarded jealously and seldom infringed except, on the odd occasion, by accident. The League's definition of an amateur as a cricketer who 'receives no remuneration over and above his actual out-of-pocket expenses' may be open to abuse but is bolstered by a frank acknowledgement that he may also 'be recompensed within reason for loss of wages when engaged in recognized matches'. There, surely, is a definition to be admired and seldom have there been occasions when the League's Management Committee have had to sit in judgement on any player. There are also no widespread obstacles to an amateur's qualifications although it is laid down and rigidly observed that no amateur be allowed to play with more than one club in any one season until his application for a transfer has been examined and approved at top official level. On the other hand there is a strictness out of the ordinary in another rule which makes it impossible for amateurs to receive collections or talent money awards for meritorious performances.

Sunderland appear to claim the major share of championship honours but they have by no means monopolized the scene and on at least two occasions, in 1907 and in 1913 play-offs were necessary. The League's handbook pays no attention and certainly no tribute to outstanding individual performances but there has been some sterling cricket and some fine players in what is a highly competitive league.

Around Tyneside it is frequently said that cricketers are the forgotten sportsmen but the activities of the Northumberland League for more than thirty years give the lie to this. Certainly there is no lack of skill or endeavour about the standard of cricket in a league that is closely linked with the Northumberland County Cricket Club. There are more than thirty clubs in membership which provides a cross-section of the area's sporting community. In recent years the League, in common with others up and down the country, has had to combat ever increasing counter attractions and ever rising costs and although crowds may be smaller and gate receipts lower than expected there is no lack of enthusiasm among either players or officials. Consequently there is no great danger to organization that embraces five divisions at senior and junior level and alongside its annual battles for championship honours provides some exciting and often closely-fought battles for the Wilson (knock-out) Cup. Although professionalism has usually been on a modest scale one comes across some well-known names in the League Handbook and when listening to the reminiscences of officials and club followers.

Eddie Phillipson, the former Lancashire bowler, spent some time in the League and so, too, did Stan Worthington, the Derbyshire and England all-rounder who was also for several years coach to the Lancashire County Cricket Club. Leslie Townsend was another Derbyshire player with Northumberland League background and Jack Oakes, one of the Sussex cricketing brothers, also left his mark in the League. One of the best batsmen was undoubtedly 'Laddie' Liddell whose record, in the League and with the county side, is comparable to that of any body else anywhere else in the world of league cricket. Of him it has always been said that figures, outstanding as they were, were never a true yardstick of his ability. How true this is of most of the best players! R. W. Smithson, of South Northumberland, had an outstanding season in 1961 when he skippered both his club and his county and averaged 61 in Minor County cricket and 91 in club cricket. Gerry Knox of Tynemouth was also a player of note for his county, his club and his league, and could usually be expected to average around the half-century mark for each innings and in each sphere.

Unfortunately when Knox went south to Lancashire he failed to make the grade at top level but maybe he was a victim as much of circumstances and of a lack of opportunity for he reached Old Trafford when Lancashire cricket was in the doldrums and had to fight his own way in a side that frequently lacked balance from the batting, bowling and captaincy point of view. Knox, nonetheless, left behind a belief that had circumstances been different he would undoubtedly have proved yet another cricketer of merit from the North-East. He was one of a vast band of eager young players who have a harder than usual fight for recognition because they come from a quarter that seldom gets more than a passing mention when league cricket is being discussed. This is wrong, for in the North-East there is good league cricket and a great reservoir of cricketing talent. It is a measure of its promise that when, as happened two or three years ago, famous players like the West Indies Test stars, Rohan Kanhai and Lance Gibbs migrated to the area, they were by no means allowed to have things all their own way. Gibbs pays tribute to the excellence of the area's many promising and punishing batsmen and Kanhai has gone on record by insisting he had to work harder for his runs in the North-East than he was forced to do in the Northern League.

Chapter 19

The South of England

There is a mistaken impression in the Greater London area, if not in a much wider sphere, that league cricket means professional cricket. It means, of course, nothing of the kind. Some of the best league cricket in the North is amateur cricket. Professionals lend a touch of spice to the game but it is only when the paid player establishes and maintains a supremacy that any real danger arises and if the amateur standard is good as it undoubtedly is in the South of England there is little danger of the professional monopolizing the scene. He can quite easily be kept out of league cricket. All it needs is a majority decision for his presence is always by invitation and there is no other way he can burst upon the scene. Professionalism, if so desired, can always be controlled, as so many leagues in the North have established.

But it is fair to ask if the club cricketer in the South has any real objection to playing with or against a professional. It happens almost every week-end when the club player contributes his quota to the benefit fund of a county cricketer and although the first-class game now makes no distinction between the amateur and the professional it was undoubtedly at its strongest when the twain played side by side to the mutual benefit of not only the players but also the watching public and the game itself. I may well be wrong but surely in the formation of the Surrey Clubs Championship there is much to suggest the beginnings of league cricket in the Greater London area and I hope the efforts of Raman Subba Row, the former Surrey and England batsman, and his colleagues will bear fruit and that, in the not too far distant future, league cricket will be able to proclaim it is nation-wide in its organisation as well as outlook. I gather from Subba Row, that the founding of the association was not achieved without difficulty. The Club

M

Cricket Conference was, not surprisingly, suspicious of the move but the fact that discussions beginning in 1966 between five Surrey club captains eventually led to an inaugural meeting in the September of that year to consider and formally approve plans for the founding of the Surrey Clubs Championship was a bold and successful move. When the association began its life it wisely put its case before the Club Cricket Conference and slowly but surely persuaded them to be tolerant to their views. It was a great step forward when, in March, 1968, after a full year of negotiation the Conference agreed to recognize the new body and amend its rules to permit them to retain membership and still experiment with their competitive brand of cricket.

Under the shrewd chairmanship of Subba Row the major obstacle was cleared and in the first year of its life seventeen clubs took part, playing in first and second divisions. Sutton won the senior championship with Purley taking the second division title. More important still, others saw the promise of this new brand of club cricket and at the end of the inaugural season there were ten additional clubs making application for places in the 1970 season. Wisely the Championship Committee has allowed the applications to lie on the table for discussion at the 1969 annual meeting and, in view of the experience gained in a further season's playing, will discuss the possible introduction of the new clubs for the 1971 season. I applaud the decision to make haste slowly. There was no desire on the part of Subba Row or any of his committee colleagues and supporters to force a split in the Club Cricket Conference ranks and their main object has been to introduce competitive cricket on a gradual scale. Whether they succeed or not, and failure surely is not to be contemplated, the bold experiment has got under way with a minimum of hostility and a welcome lack of controversy. There are surely many exiled northerners now living and working in the south of England who would like to see the Surrey Clubs Championship prosper because it is to them the beginning of league cricket in territory previously totally opposed to such a move.

Outside of the Greater London area there has been much that is similar to league cricket in most parts of the South of England.

Competitive cricket has certainly been played in Devon and Cornwall for a long time and recent sponsorship has served to encourage the clubs concerned to indulge in professionalism and battle for trophies. There are several smaller cricketing organisations on league lines in Essex and parts of Sussex, while Cambridgeshire shares with Norfolk a similar trend to cricket on league lines. Indeed the absence of big crowds and highly paid professionals should not imply that league cricket does not exist in every part of England: for what is league cricket? Simply club cricket streamlined by rules and regulations and braced with the competitive spirit.

Chapter 20

Wales and Scotland

League cricket in Wales may lack some of the competitive element so much in evidence in England but one cannot leave the Principality out of the general pattern of things. The country is divided into two major organizations who control, or rather guide the week-end cricketing activities of the many keen and talented players to be found throughout Wales. Looking south to start with, the South Wales and Monmouthshire Cricket Association casts a wide net and is closely linked with the Glamorganshire County Cricket Club inasmuch as it allows the county to be represented on its Management Committee and also does much by way of providing young players for first-class cricket. The Association was founded in 1926 and continued until the outbreak of World War II. There was, however, no lack of cricket played on a 'friendly' basis and when the war was over the Association sprang quickly back into its stride. A great step forward was taken in 1960 when promotion and relegation issues were instituted and four divisions provided some thrilling and often highly skilled cricket.

Never afraid to experiment, the Association was one of the first of the cricketing bodies to introduce time-limit cricket without losing in its modernization plans the real desire to play the game as intensely and sportingly as always. Professionalism has always been permitted but few clubs have branched out on any wide scale, the general belief being that the league cricket professional was far better employed at the nets encouraging and correcting the faults of the young rather than producing fantastic figures with bat and ball in the middle. In the main league cricket in South Wales has been for the amateurs but the Glamorganshire County Cricket Club have, of course, benefited from being able not only to spot the up and coming batsmen and bowlers but also to send out their experienced players to advise and encourage a standard of play that might well surprise those who judge their league cricket by Lancashire and Yorkshire standards. The Ebbw Vale club has usually set the pattern with regard to any big-name signings and at one time Charles Hallows, the Lancashire and England left-hander, was a club professional and later Harold Gimblett, the Somerset big hitter, also joined the club, but the general tendency is to employ the men who can be spared from the first-class cricket scene with Glamorgan. In this respect Brian Edrich and Alan Rees went out into the hills and the valleys to play outstanding cricket for a time. Edrich, a bonny fighter with the bat, once highlighted the month of August with two superb centuries on behalf of the Maesteg Cricket Club, and Rees also produced several centuries of style and power when playing for BFT., one of the many thriving works clubs in Welsh league cricket.

Under limited overs or time limit conditions it is not possible to point to men who have amassed runs in the manner of their Lancashire or Yorkshire counterparts or taken wickets with the power of the many world-famous players who have been tempted into Northern league cricket but nonetheless the Saturday afternoon game in South Wales has much to attract both the spectator and the player and it is significant that in recent years there have been more and better recruits to the first-class scene in Glamorgan than ever before. Jeff and Alan Jones are two Glamorgan cricketers who demonstrate this in impressive manner and Wilfred Wooller, the versatile secretary of the county club, has frequently paid tribute to the growing number of recruits now coming off the league cricket 'pipe line' in South Wales. The major reason for satisfaction is that in the not too distant future Glamorgan will be able and encouraged to field a team of Welsh born players.

Certainly with upwards of fifty clubs in the Association and at least as many functioning outside its sphere of influence the future of Welsh cricket is assured. Clubs of the calibre of Ebbw Vale, Neath, Llanelly, Swansea and Gowerton represent the city and town influence and from the workshops and factories of suc h cricketing organizations as Grovesend Works, SCW (Port Talbot), Briton Ferry Steelworks and Metal Box (Neath) are bound to come not only a steady stream of good young players but also the men with administrative flair. And, perhaps above all, the spectators who watch the Association's matches, week in and week out, summer by summer, are also the men and the women who are going to give the lie to the all-too-frequent challenge that cricket is losing its mass appeal. It is simply not true and any man who cares to look at the South Wales and Monmouthshire Association will realize it.

In North Wales, the North Wales Cricket Association has a long record to be proud of and embraces clubs in six counties – Anglesey, Caernarvonshire, Denbighshire, Flintshire, Merionethshire and Montgomeryshire: in all there are over 120 clubs and works organizations playing cricket. Formed over forty years ago the Association has had its problems – what cricketing body has not – but has surmounted them by self-sacrifice and an almost fanatical desire to keep the game going at all times. The Association differs from its Lancashire and Yorkshire counterparts and, indeed, from its South Wales ally, because it also believes in and does much to stir up county rivalry in its own sphere. In addition to its weekly cricket at club level the Association, taking over from the old North Wales County body, now organizes and certainly enjoys an inter-county competition within its own borders – where the accent is mainly upon amateur cricket and good amateur cricket at that. Professionalism is permitted but few clubs can afford it and what money is available for outside help to the Association clubs is modest. This is no handicap. North Wales cricket is happy cricket and friendly cricket. But that does not mean it is without the competitive element. Indeed, if it were possible for some of the North Wales clubs to play their Lancashire or Yorkshire counterparts the results might well astonish.

No doubt one of these days the matter will be put to the test, but it is within my own recollection that the Wrexham Cricket Club at one time paid several visits to Middleton and gave the Central Lancashire League side some very anxious, indeed embarrassing moments. League cricket in North Wales is superbly organized with the sort of fervour and favour that makes Welsh sport so highly inflammable on international occasions. Certainly the standard of play is high and the standard of pitch and enclosure is also a matter for congratulation with a special mark for enterprise going to the Colwyn Cricket Club whose ground at Rhos-on-Sea is one of the best in the British Isles. For years it has been the scene of an annual Cricketing Festival that has drawn the best players from most of the cricketing countries of the world and now it is also the annual venue for at least one Glamorganshire first-class fixture each summer. Soon there could be more first-class cricket in North Wales: for crowds are big and playing conditions second to none.

It would not be unfair to nominate Colwyn Bay as the focal centre of cricket in North Wales but not all cricket played in this vast area is, strictly speaking, league cricket, yet it is played and organized on lines so successful in the North of England that few in Wales will object to being classed as league cricket supporters. It is a little unusual to find that the names of officials are better known than the names of players, but almost all who worked for cricket were good batsmen or bowlers before they became administrators and this is the secret of good cricket at club level. For a man to play for ten, fifteen or twenty years, and then turn his attention to committee work and administrative problems is undoubtedly the recipe for success, and North Wales is stronger than most areas in this respect. The foremost amongst them have been, and in many cases still are, connected with the Colwyn Bay Cricket Club, the name of P. G. Gadd being outstanding in terms of service on and off the field. R. H. Moore, the former Hampshire captain, did much to enlighten the cricketing scene at the Bay and elsewhere for many years and, from the professional point of view the Colwyn club were ideally served for many years by Alf Cassley, the man who learned his cricket at Middleton, moved over to Stand in the Lancashire and Cheshire League and, rejecting several invitations to sample Lancashire League cricket at far better money than he obtained elsewhere, eventually finished his career in North Wales. There his canny spin bowling and hard-hitting brand of batsmanship are valued alongside his coaching and encouragement of young players.

Today, in face of fiercer than ever counter-attraction and rapid switches in population and labour the North Wales Cricket Association proudly proclaims that its principles remain the same as when it was founded in the more leisurely 1920s. They are: the organization of inter-county cricket between the six constituent counties; the selection of teams to play representative cricket and to co-ordinate and assist all the counties and all the clubs in all matters relating to the promoting and development of cricket. Are these ideals any different from those that obtain throughout all league cricket? The phraseology may be different but the ultimate object is the same, and whilst league cricket in Wales may not be so well-known as that in the North of England it is, nevertheless, equally important and well worthy of encouragement.

It is often said that Scotland is not cricket conscious but there is a lot of cricket played in Scotland, and, although in terms of public support and first-class standards it is a minority sport, Scotland cannot be omitted from the cricketing picture. There has been league cricket there for many years and in the 1920s I know of several Lancashire league clubs who annually made pilgrimage to sample and enjoy the cricket played in the various Scottish counties. Quite often a club had to strengthen its resources to take on the major Scottish clubs with any real hope of success and from the point of view of enthusiasm and refusal to bow to the often overwhelming demand for football there is nothing in sport quite to rival the determination of the Scot who is fond of cricket. The East League, and the Border League link up with the Western Union and the Strathmore Union; then there is the Scottish County Championship which features representative teams of Perthshire, Forfarshire, West Lothian, Aberdeenshire, Fife, Stirling County and Clackmannon. The very names give the lie to the general belief Scotland is 'heathen' country when it comes to cricket. The East League comprises fourteen clubs including Stenhousemuir who won the championship in 1968, Edinburgh University, Heriot's FP., Melville College FP., Watsonians, and

Grange, the bottom-of-the-table club whose percentage in 1968 was a modest 16.6 but will undoubtedly be better in the future.

The West of Scotland club took the championship of the Western Union in 1968 and won thirteen out of their sixteen championship engagements but only just managed to ward off Clydesdale who were winners outright of a dozen games. These two clubs were the successes of the season, whereas poor Kelburne finished at the bottom of the league table and failed to win even one of its sixteen matches, picking up only two points throughout the whole of the season. Selkirk, winning ten matches out of eleven, took the Border League honours in 1968 but there again it would be unfair and unsporting not to mention the wholehearted efforts of the Langholm Cricket Club players and officials. They went through the summer losing match after match and in the end could show nothing for their efforts except twelve played, twelve lost, and not a point to lessen the pain! Yet they never once failed to turn out a full side and frequently had the opposition in trouble.

Strathmore were the champions of the Strathmore Union section in 1968 with Arbroath United at the foot of the table, and in the Scottish Counties League Perthshire well earned the championship with Clackmannon holding the wooden spoon. Professionalism is permissable in Scottish league cricket: Wilfred Rhodes frequently moved from Yorkshire to Scotland for a summer's cricketing engagement in the twilight of his career and so, too, did Schofield Haigh, another redoubtable Yorkshire cricketer. In more recent years Rohan Kanhai of the West Indies, Alimuddin of Pakistan, and Ashley Mallett of Australia, have all spent seasons in Scottish cricket and pay ample tribute to the high standard of play, the enthusiasm of the club followers, and the excellence of their many grounds, rural and industrial.

One must not forget another Scottish League – one that appears to get little of the spotlight. Nonetheless the North of Scotland League provides excellent cricket in the Ross and Cromarty, Inverness-shire and along the south shores of the Moray Firth and maintains the country's reputation for taking cricket with all seriousness and at all times.

I recall the late Jimmy Fleming, who held a passionate faith in

Scottish cricket, telling me some wonderful stories of the games and the men who played in them twenty or thirty years ago. One of his best concerned a well-known Scottish cricketer, a big hitter and a steady drinker, who, on going in to bat against a touring team of league cricketers from Lancashire, played two terrific hook shots, literally off his eyebrows hitting the ball out of the ground when a young and ambitious fast bowler with more ambition than good sense greeted him with two fiery bumpers. 'Hold on, a wee moment, laddie,' said the batsman. 'Ah'm not seeing 'em well, as yet.' And the worthy local proceeded to slip his false teeth into a handkerchief and hand them to the umpire with a plea 'Look after mi' biters for an hour or so, Jock, ah'll be teachin this young man a lesson.' And, apparently he did, getting a quick half-century and collecting his dentures before he retired to the pavilion and the bar for a thirst quencher.

Jimmy also loved to recount the story of the visiting cricketer who found himself without accommodation in a remote Scottish village one night after staying too long in the bar at the end of the match. Left behind, whether by accident or design when the touring coach drove off without checking its passengers, the stranded one returned to his drinking companions. One of them offered to put him up for the night saying: 'We'll find you a bed, dinna fret.' They did and when morning dawned the stranger enquired about the extent of his indebtedness. 'Forget it, mon, Jeannie and I were happy to help,' was the reply. But the stranded one was insistent and in the end his host capitulated. 'If tha must, tha must, but we want none o'your money. Gie the wee bairns a pound each and forget it.' The wee bairns totalled six!

It is in the nature of things that club cricket and league cricket there lead directly into representative cricket and few counties can resist the invitation to entertain or be entertained by Scotland at some time or other. Lord's, of course, is the ground for the annual MCC v. Scotland match and the men who come south to represent their country are the same who enjoy cricket in the leagues.

Chapter 21

The Umpires

Umpires are so often the forgotten men of cricket, and they are the worst paid, but they have the power to make or mar a game and deprive both the players and the spectators of enjoyment. In league cricket there are no more conscientious officials: they are often the sole judges not only of conditions for play but also of the fairness of it. And whilst in most of the major leagues up and down the country there is a degree of payment for umpires, quite often their job is only a labour of love. The majority of league cricket umpires are old players who cannot tear themselves away from the scene of battle; but whether a man has played the game or not to accept the duties of an umpire in League cricket is to acknowledge one's regard for the game, for he is subject to far more criticism than the players. Week after week in the Central Lancashire League, as a young and as an experienced player, I marvelled at the umpires' composure. If he gave a batsman out lbw he was sure to arouse the wrath of the crowd. If he no-balled a popular professional he was equally sure to be the butt of the spectators. But when, and it frequently happened, he gave a decision against an amateur who was enjoying himself with either bat or ball the volume of criticism swelled to tremendous proportions. The umpire in league cricket simply cannot win. His decisions, given without fear and favour except in the very smallest minority of cases, may please one but annoy another and yet at the risk of being temporarily unpopular with all those around him the umpire makes up his mind and acts accordingly.

It is a task for men of the toughest fibre and I like nothing better than the story of the old Central Lancashire League umpire who had the audacity to no-ball the great Sydney Barnes four times in one over. It happened at Rochdale after the first World

War, and Barnes was the home club professional who had already captured two or three cheap wickets. Barnes was no-balled off the first ball of the over. The second went down unchallenged but then, to the consternation of the crowd and the annoyance of the world famous bowler there came two successive cries of 'no-ball' and the great man stopped in his tracks. He came and looked at the line he was judged to have overstepped, marked another an inch or two behind and was then called again. It was not possible to hear the conversation from the pavilion side but I was later assured that it went something like this: Barnes demanded to know what he was doing wrong and the umpire boldly asserted 'tha's scraping t'line and tha's not going to get away wi' it.' 'But, my man, I am getting ten pounds a week to entertain this crowd,' said the aggrieved Barnes. 'Ah knows that. Ahm only getting ten bob but ahm bloody boss and until tha toes line tha doesna finish t'over,' replied the umpire. And so it went on. The great Sydney Barnes sent down ten deliveries before he satisfied a hawk-eyed umpire for ever after accused of taking the mickey out of a great bowler. There in a nutshell is the secret of league cricket, the game in which the famous and the unknown rub shoulders and come to battle.

By and large, the man who volunteers for duty as an umpire in league cricket is as fair and as honest as the men who play it; and if it were possible to undertake an opinion poll of all league cricket followers, officials, players and spectators, there would be an overwhelming majority praising rather than condemning the work of the men in the middle who officiate, in the words of the creed that heads the notepaper of the Central Lancashire League Umpires' Association, 'without fear or favour'. Almost without exception every league worthy of its name has an Umpires' Association; and they work in close co-operation to ensure that the game is not marred by the decisions that have to be given upon appeal. Years ago I took the late Frank Chester to Rochdale to lecture and examine the Central Lancashire umpires, and he came away convinced that the league had no cause for concern either at the standard or the understanding of the men who officiated. He said that none of the umpires he spoke to were officiating for what they could get out of it but obviously for what they could put into it.

It is because of this loyalty that incidents are few and far between in league cricket. Not that there is never any trouble: there must, even in the best regulated leagues, be occasions when the League Committee has to sit in judgement upon complaints brought either against or by an umpire. It calls for the wisdom of Solomon in deciding the rights and the wrongs of some cases but if the League officials give the umpire their full backing, as they almost unanimously do, they are on the right path. In league cricket, as in first-class cricket, there comes a time when a batsman or a bowler is far from satisfied with an umpiring decision. But, as one old professional always used to insist, 'It's no use moaning. One day tha may get a bad 'un, but next tha'll be in luck, so tak it as it comes.' Such logic may not strictly be legal but it is the basis for fair play and was usually observed to the letter in the league cricket that I played.

At present many leagues have difficulty gathering together a full complement of umpires and it is not unusual for some club official to be roped in for duty at the last minute on a Saturday or Sunday afternoon; but in the major leagues such happenings are rare and there is always a ready response to the annual appeal for old players to rally round and stay in the game as umpires. Add to these old-timers a steady flow of men who turn to umpiring because they did not make the grade as players and you have a reservoir of manpower to be freely tapped. Yet the Derbyshire and Cheshire League was bold enough, in the 1969 season, to enrol a woman on their registered list of umpires. And why not? This particular lady had learned the rules, answered all the examination demands and stood the test of questions fired at her when interviewed. She will obviously at times have to close her ears to some uncricket-like language but if she can cope with the players and administer cricketing justice without fear or favour she may well have opened up a new source of supply for the leagues in difficulties.

Chapter 22

The League Cricket Conference

Most leagues have their own county associations to help them sort out the problems that arise from time to time in the running of the game but in 1962 there came the formation of the League Cricket Conference, the brain child of a Staffordshireman, Doug Schofield, of Tunstall, the honorary secretary of the North Staffordshire and South Cheshire League. Mr Schofield saw the need for a national body to look after the interests of league cricket as a whole and one of the first tasks of the newly constituted body was to take over the organization of the Rothman Cup, the trophy donated by the well-known tobacco company for annual competition between the leagues in the country at representative level. First played for in 1965 the Cup now attracts entries from all the major leagues except the Lancashire League who, as yet, cannot see their way to providing the time or the venues to play without interference with their own league fixtures. Sunday cricket has, of course, been the means of drawing into the competition representatives from an area beginning at the Scottish border and stretching down to Birmingham in the Midlands. The first winners were the North Staffordshire and South Cheshire League, followed, in 1966, by the Bradford League and then, in 1967 and 1968 by the Lincolnshire County League. The Competition has done a great amount of good in cementing the bonds of friendship between the leagues and their officials.

At the moment there are some 23 leagues in membership of the Conference who meet annually, usually at Scarborough, at the end of each season, to discuss and debate topics that have created problems or given rise to misunderstanding throughout the year.

The Conference has wisely not attempted or contemplated any interference with the individual rights of their member leagues or suggested ways and means of standardizing any cricketing custom. But there will come a time when, through the united efforts of the leagues in membership, it will undoubtedly be able to exercise an authority and perhaps introduce measures for the benefit of league cricket as a whole.

Certainly there is a spirit of comradeship and mutual co-operation that hints at a happy and brighter future for all those who play or organize their cricket at league level. When the time comes, as inevitably it must come, for all branches of cricket to stand together the leagues, with their own county organizations and now the League Cricket Conference, will not lack the ways and the means to put their views before the people who matter most in the pattern that is to be cricket of the future. That the leagues have an important part to play goes without question. That they are well prepared to meet the challenge is evident. That they do so with the well-being of cricket uppermost in their minds is also essential. I have a feeling league cricket will not be found wanting. It has stood the test of time and lived through too many years to be beaten in a crisis. And remember that league cricket is essentially club cricket with rules and regulations and a tinge of discipline that has been fostered on hard work and a desire to be loyal to a British way of life. It surely is a formula for successful sport.

Chapter 23

Looking Forward

Glancing back over a lifetime of league cricket has revived nostalgic memories of happy days in the sun, of great players, some famous, some unknown outside their local sphere of activity. It has revived memories of good fellowship and tremendous sporting endeavour, of thrilling victories and disappointing defeats, but above all it has restored my faith in the future of cricket at week-end level. There are complications. It would be idle to deny that league cricket faces problems. Some are of its own making, others are forced upon officials and players by the march of time and the rapidly changing world in which we live. None of the problems are insurmountable given the goodwill, the right spirit, and the determination to win through as our fathers and grandfathers before us did. That the cost of the upkeep of league cricket is getting higher and higher there can be no denying. But wages are also rising and if there is such a thing as value for money it remains as true today as ever it did that one volunteer worker is worth two who measure their endeavour by the size of a pay packet or the hours on the clock.

There need be no fear for the future of league cricket so long as the old spirit of comradeship and determination to succeed persists. It is years now since the players and officials of the Heywood Cricket Club trudged around the town dragging and playing a barrel organ to raise the cash to meet the weekly wage bill. They gathered in a mere thirty shillings one night, a princely £30 the next, and the crisis was overcome. It was the same sturdy spirit of independence and proud sporting heritage that produced the story of the famous professional who was bowled first ball on a bright and breezy day in the Lancashire League. Quick as the wind the old-timer picked up the bails and replaced them on the stumps as he turned to the umpire and said: 'It's windy to-day, umpire.' 'Aye, mon, 'tis. Stick to thi cap as tha reaches yon pavilion,' was the retort of the white-coated official not to be caught out by any trick of gamesmanship. It is a simple story but it illustrates the charm and the humour that has enabled league cricket to survive from one generation to another.

It is the self-same spirit of determination to live on that will guarantee its future. There are still men, and women too, who are prepared to work hard and make sacrifices to keep the local cricket club in action. There are still players who are determined to do battle with the famous professionals and come out on top. Crowds may be smaller and playing standards may have slumped a little, although this is purely a matter of opinion, but by and large league cricket is still healthy. It will not die because the desire to continue is so vibrant a part of the true sportsman. Maybe there has been too much interference from officials. League cricket, like its first-class neighbour, has tended recently to breed a race of administrators many of them former players who have believed it their job to 'streamline' the game. Sooner or later, and let us hope it is sooner, the truth will dawn upon them that cricket is made or marred by those who play it and not by those who administrate for it. The problems of the game, at week-end level just as much as at the higher level, cannot be solved by changing the rules or imposing new conditions. The solution lies with the batsmen, the bowlers, and the fieldsmen. The sooner they are left alone to solve the problems on the field of play the sooner the problems off it will disappear.

There may well be need for changes. I visualize a demand for the 'nationalization' of the league game, played in county leagues of several divisions with promotion and relegation battles to be fought and won. But basically there is nothing wrong with league cricket that good weather and the commonsense of those who play it cannot put right. League cricketers are the 'Do It Yourself' brigade of sport. Where there is a will there is always a way. The past has been glorious. The future is still bright.

N

Epilogue - The 1969 Season

Once again it was the professionals who hit the headlines in league cricket in 1969 – yet, as always, the amateurs provided the background support without which no club and no league can prosper. In the Lancashire League, for example, six amateur batsmen topped the 500-run mark as against seven professionals equally proficient with the bat, and six unpaid bowlers claimed fifty or more wickets against eleven equally successful professionals, while in the Central Lancashire League the figures were similarly impressive with two young amateur bowlers, Peter Syddall (Castleton Moor) and Peter Wilson (Milnrow) breaking club records with 70 and 80 victims respectively. Yet it was Neil Hawke, the Australian Test bowler and Nelson professional, who was persistently in the news from the Lancashire League point of view. Hawke, returning after one season's absence whilst touring England with the Australian side, captured 112 wickets and hit 582 runs – and Nelson regained the championship they had yielded to Rishton in 1968.

In the Central Lancashire League Radcliffe won an exciting battle for the championship and did not have to depend overmuch on their professional, Cec Abrahams, one of several coloured South African cricketers now in the leagues. Abrahams had the rather modest returns of 67 wickets and 573 runs but was fortunate in having some good amateur support with Derek Johnson, a sound all-rounder producing 520 runs and 40 wickets, and Bill Holt proving another useful bowler with 42 wickets at reasonable cost. But for steady all-round cricket there was no better player than the Heywood professional, Colin Lever, whose haul of 86 wickets and aggregate of 670 runs kept his club in the fight for the championship until the last two matches. Bob Cooke, a former Manchester Association amateur, made an impressive debut in the professional ranks with 630 runs and 81 wickets on behalf of

Stockport who won the Wood Cup, the Second Division title and the Aggregate Trophy with a young side of great possibilities.

In the Midlands Moseley were the Birmingham League champions and in Yorkshire Bingley took the title in the First Division of the Bradford League with Farsley running away with the Second Division championship and earning promotion along with Pudsey St Lawrence who added one more achievement to their cricketing record when Ray Illingworth, a native of the town and a onetime playing member of the club, successfully captained England against the West Indies and New Zealand – a feat recognized by his club at the end of the season when Illingworth returned 'home' and was given a civic reception. Professionalism is now practised on a modest scale in the Bradford League and also in the Birmingham League but in the Midland averages it was not difficult to spot a couple of names once prominent in first-class cricketing circles. Alan Townsend, the former Warwickshire all-rounder, hit 490 runs for Mitchell & Butler but came third in the averages to J. F. Smith (West Bromwich Dartmouth, 552 runs for an average of 55.20) and P. Harris (Kidderminster, 414 runs for an average of 41.40). With the ball Roly Jenkins, of Worcestershire and England, captured 47 wickets on behalf of West Bromwich Dartmouth, with his still bewildering mixture of leg-breaks, googlies and off-spinners.

The battle for the Rothman Cup was keen and well supported, with the North Staffordshire and South Cheshire League proving the winners in a closely contested final against the Northern League on the Great Chell ground in Staffordshire. The home side hit up 155 and dismissed the opposition for 126 to take the trophy for the second and probably last time for the sponsors, satisfied with their efforts to bring the various leagues together on the field of play, have now withdrawn their sponsorship.

In the five years of the competition the North Staffordshire and South Cheshire League were victorious as well in 1965, the Bradford League were successful in 1966, and in 1967 and 1968 the Lincolnshire County League achieved a well merited 'double'. The withdrawal of Rothman's support does not mean the end of the competition and throughout the winter League Cricket Conference officials have been working hard to ensure the continuance of this highly popular tournament under a different name and sponsorship. The 'vital statistics' of the season included:

LANCASHIRE LEAGUE

Club	P	W	L	D	Pts.	Professional	Runs	Av.	Wkts.	Av.
Nelson	26	13	3	10	69	N Hawke	582	36.37	112	7.07
East Lancashire	26	9	2	15	59	P Trimborn	407	27.13	90	10.9
Burnley	26	11	6	9	57	L Mayne	334	21.03	96	12.10
Rishton	26	9	3	14	54	M L Jaisimha	644	26.83	40	19.62
Ramsbottom	26	6	4	16	49	R Nadkarni	506	26.63	75	10.32
Colne	26	7	5	14	48	R Ramnerace	708	28.32	81	14.32
Enfield	26	8	5	13	44	D Abed	424	22.31	105	10.40
Accrington	26	5	5	16	43	P Swart	738	35.14	67	12.66
Bacup	26	6	4	16	43	I Brayshaw	836	34.83	59	15.29
Church	26	7	9	10	40	G Abbas	755	34.31	22	33.77
Haslingden	26	4	8	14	36	W English	592	26.90	66	13.80
Todmorden	26	1	10	15	26	R Majeit	437	20.80	28	20.60
Rawtenstall	26	1	12	13	23	D Renneberg	253	14.05	65	14.90
Lowerhouse	26	3	9	14	21	D Sparks	89	3.87	78	12.11

CENTRAL LANCASHIRE LEAGUE

Club	P	W	L	D	Pts.	Professional	Runs	Av.	Wkts.	Av.
Radcliffe	26	14	5	7*	69	C Abrahams	573	23.87	67	13.13
Royton	26	12	7	7*	67	C Watson	457	25.38	74	10.20
Stockport	26	12	8	6	67	R Cooke	630	26.25	81	10.62
Heywood	26	12	9	5	63	C Lever	670	27.91	86	7.82
Milnrow	26	13	6	7*	63	K Grieves	585	30.78	49	12.18
Castleton Moor	26	11	11	4	59	J Howarth	155	9.63	74	11.16
Walsden	26	10	10	6*	57	C Wright	200	9.52	116	9.51
Werneth	26	12	8	6*	55	D February	253	14.05	53	16.60
Ashton	26	9	10	7*	54	K Gillhouley	250	13.15	42	15.19
Middleton	26	10	10	6*	52	J Swinburne	193	10.72	51	11.39
Oldham	26	8	14	4*	42	M J Hilton	140	7.00	60	14.93
Littleborough	26	6	13	7	38	D Carter	452	20.50	101	10.90
Crompton	26	6	14	6	33	C Depeiza	588	34.58	47	15.61
Rochdale	26	7	14	5	32	G Abed	552	26.28	58	15.00

* Denotes two points for tied games.

BIRMINGHAM LEAGUE

Club	P	W	L	D	Pts.
Moseley	18	10	0	8	52
West Brom. Dartmouth	18	7	1	10	41
Dudley	18	4	2	12	32
Aston Unity	18	4	3	11	31
Smethwick	18	4	5	8	27
Walsall	18	2	5	11	24
Kidderminster	18	1	0	17	22
Mitchell & Bulter	18	0	5	13	19
Stourbridge	18	1	5	12	19
Old Hill	18	0	6	12	16

BRADFORD LEAGUE

First Division	P	W	L	D	Pts.	Second Division	P	W	L	D	Pts
Bingley	22	9	2	11	58	Farsley	22	12	3	7	6
Spen Victoria	22	9	3	10	55	Pudsey St. Lawrence	22	8	4	10	5
Undercliffe	22	6	3	13	47	Laisterdyke	22	8	5	9	5
Idle	22	5	4	13	44	Yeadon	22	8	3	11	5
Bankfoot	22	5	4	13	44	Windhill	22	7	6	9	4
Lightcliffe	22	6	5	11	41	Salts	22	5	6	11	4
Bradford	22	5	3	14	39	Keighley	22	5	5	12	3
East Brierley	22	5	6	11	36	Lidgett Green	22	5	6	11	3
Hartshead Moor	22	5	6	11	36	Queensbury	22	3	6	13	3
Bowling Old Lane	22	4	7	11	31	Baildon	22	4	7	11	3
Saltaire	22	1	8	13	20	Brighouse	22	2	7	13	2
Eccleshill	22	1	10	11	18	Great Horton	22	1	10	11	1

NORTH STAFFORDSHIRE AND SOUTH CHESHIRE LEAGUE

Club	P	W	L	D	Pts.
Longton	22	8	2	12	49
Bignall End	22	6	2	14	43
Leek	22	7	3	12	43
Nantwich	22	7	4	11	39
Knypersley	22	5	4	13	38
Newcastle and Hartshill	22	5	4	13	38
Porthill Park	22	5	4	13	37
Stone	22	5	4	13	36
Norton	22	4	5	13	30
Crewe LMR	22	2	6	14	26
Sneyd	22	1	9	12	18
Great Chell	22	1	9	12	17

NORTH STAFFORDSHIRE AND DISTRICT LEAGUE

Senior A

Club	P	W	L	D	Pts.
Cheadle	18	10	0	8	48
Caverswall	18	6	3	9	33
Burslem	18	6	6	6	30
Kidsgrove	18	5	5	8	28
Audley	18	5	7	6	26
Crewe R – R.	18	4	4	10	26
Blythe M.	18	3	3	12	24
Betley	18	3	7	8	20
Congleton	18	2	4	12	20
Sandyford	18	2	7	9	17

Senior B

Club	P	W	L	D	Pts.
Simplex	18	10	5	3	43
Silverdale	18	6	2	10	34
Boltons	18	6	5	7	31
Michelin	18	6	7	5	29
Scot Hay	18	6	7	5	29
E.C.C.	18	5	5	8	28
Fodens	18	5	7	6	26
Ashcombe Park	18	3	9	6	18

SCOTTISH COUNTY CHAMPIONSHIP

Club	P	W	L	D	Pts.	%
Perthshire	8	4	0	4	36	75
Aberdeenshire	9	5	1	3	39	72
West Lothian	8	4	2	2	30	62
Fife	9	1	2	6	24	44
Clackmannan	7	2	4	1	15	35
Forfarshire	9	1	4	4	18	33
Stirling	8	0	4	4	12	25

SCOTTISH WESTERN UNION

Club	P	W	L	D	Pts.	%
Kilmarnock	14	11	1	2	24	85
Ferguslie	15	10	1	4	23	76
Uddingston	15	7	5	3	16	53
Clydesdale	15	6	3	6	15	50
West of Scotland	13	5	5	3	13	50
Polock	16	6	7	3*	13	30
Greenock	15	4	8	3*	9	30
Kelburne	14	2	6	6*	8	28
Drumpellier	14	2	8	4	5	17
Ayr	15	1	10	4	3	10

* Extra points for tied matches.

SCOTTISH BORDER LEAGUE

Club	P	W	L	D	Pts.	%
Kelso	11	10	1	0	20	90.9
Selkirk	10	9	1	0	18	90.00
Gala	11	9	2	0	18	81.8
Langholm	11	5	6	0	10	45.4
Hawick	12	3	9	0	6	25.00
Dumfries	12	3	9	0	6	25.00
St. Boswells	9	2	7	0	4	22.2
Penicuik	8	1	7	0	2	12.5

SCOTTISH EAST LEAGUE

Club	P	W	L	D	Pts.	%
Heriot's F. P.	10	8	0	2*	25	83.3
Edinburgh Academicals	10	7	0	3	24	80.00
Royal H.S. F.P.	12	7	0	5*	27	75.00
Stenhousemuir	9	5	1	3	18	66.6
Carlton	11	5	2	4	19	57.5
Edinburgh University	9	3	1	5*	15	55.5
Watsonians	11	3	2	6	15	45.4
Leith Franklin	12	3	6	3	12	33.3
Grange	8	2	4	2	8	33.3
Brunswick	11	2	6	3	9	27.2
Melville College F.P.	8	1	4	3*	6	25.00
Cupar	10	1	5	4	7	23.3
Stewart's College F.P.	9	1	5	3	6	22.2
Kirkcaldy	9	1	7	1	4	14.8
Trinity Academicals	9	1	7	1	4	14.8

* Extra points for tied matches.

SCOTTISH STRATHMORE UNION

Club	P	W	L	D	Pts.	%
Strathmore	15	11	0	4	37	82.00
Meigle	14	8	5	1	25	59.00
Mannofield XI	20	10	5	5	35	58.00
Brechin	19	9	5	5	32	56.00
Blairgowrie	17	8	6	3	27	52.00
Gordonians	16	5	5	6	21	43.00
Forthill XI	18	6	7	5	23	42.00
Aberdeen G.S. F.P.	15	4	5	6	18	40.00
Perthshire XI	19	6	9	4	22	38.00
Arbroath United	16	4	6	6	18	37.00
Coupar-Angus	17	6	10	1	19	37.00
Dundee H.S. F.P.	16	4	8	4	16	33.00
Montrose	17	3	13	1	10	19.00

Index of Clubs

Index of Players